TAKE a STAND!

TAKE *a* STAND!

Classroom Activities That Explore Philosophical Arguments That Matter to Teens

Sharon M. Kaye, Ph.D.

Library of Congress Cataloging-in-Publication Data

Names: Kaye, Sharon M., author.
Title: Take a stand! : classroom activities that explore philosophical arguments that matter to teens / Sharon Kaye.
Description: Waco, TX : Prufrock Press Inc., 2020. | Includes bibliographical references. | Summary: ""Take a Stand!" (grades 9-12) helps teens develop critical thinking skills by examining debates on issues directly relevant to their lives (that you won't find in most classroom materials)"-- Provided by publisher.
Identifiers: LCCN 2020028936 (print) | LCCN 2020028937 (ebook) | ISBN 9781646320691 (paperback) | ISBN 9781646320707 (ebook) | ISBN 9781646320868 (epub)
Subjects: LCSH: Critical thinking--Study and teaching--Activity programs. | Philosophy--Study and teaching--Activity programs. | Social history--Study and teaching--Activity programs. | Teenagers--Attitudes.
Classification: LCC LB1590.3 .K39 2020 (print) | LCC LB1590.3 (ebook) | DDC 370.15/2--dc23
LC record available at https://lccn.loc.gov/2020028936
LC ebook record available at https://lccn.loc.gov/2020028937

First published in 2020 by Prufrock Press Inc.

Published in 2021 by Routledge
605 Third Avenue, New York, NY 10017
2 Park Square, Milton Park, Abingdon, Oxon OX14 4RN

Routledge is an imprint of the Taylor & Francis Group, an informa business

Cover design by Allegra Denbo and layout design by Shelby Charette

ISBN: 9781032142272 (hbk)
ISBN: 9781646320691 (pbk)

DOI: 10.4324/9781003238393

{Table of Contents}

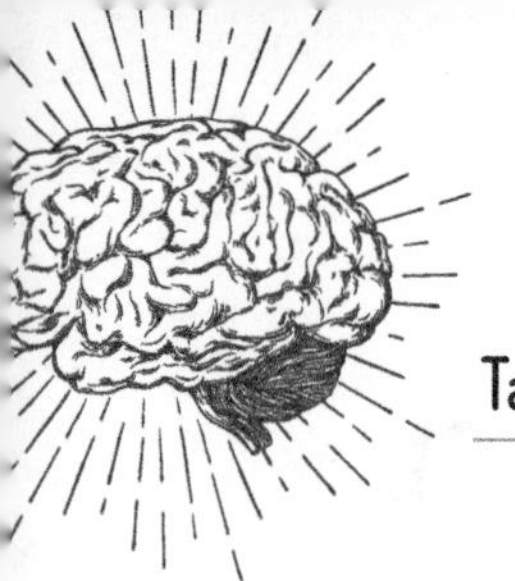

Part III: Relationships

Part IV: Sex

Acknowledgments

With special thanks to Dr. Heinrik Hellwig for editorial assistance.

Preface

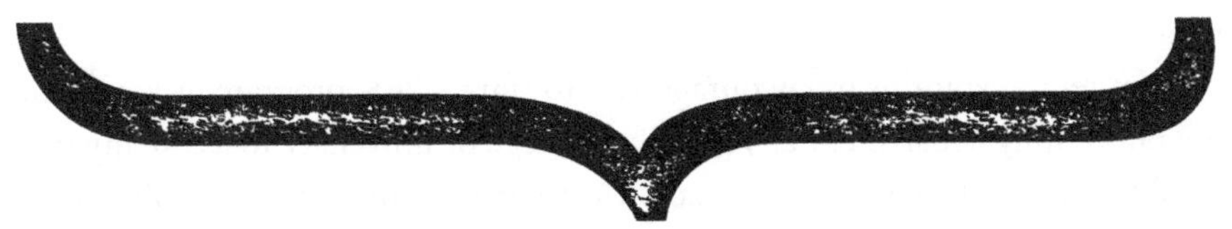

by Sharon M. Kaye

This book grew out of a program at John Carroll University (JCU) called Philosophy for Kids (P4K). P4K began in 2016 as an effort on the part of the JCU Department of Philosophy to build academic and social connections with the surrounding community. Each year, 10 undergraduate interns pair up to teach five philosophy classes in the gifted programs at three nearby public schools. Classes are held once per week for anywhere between 30 minutes to an hour.

By "teaching," I mean that the interns facilitate philosophy discussions. They are not education majors and receive no special training. Their job is made easier by the fact that they do not give homework or tests. Furthermore, the classroom teacher stays in the room to handle any classroom management issues that may arise. Still, the work the interns do is amazing. They plunge school-weary teens into the deepest questions human beings have ever asked, including:

- Who are you?
- Is the world real?
- Where does knowledge come from?
- What is the meaning of life?

These discussions are transformative. They are often the highlight of the day, the month, or the year for everyone involved.

JCU interns and their classroom teachers learn just as much from their P4K classes as their students do. Contrary to popular assumption, kids are actually very good at philosophy. The word *philosophy* comes from the Greek words for "love" and "wisdom." Young minds are full of the curiosity that breeds the love of wisdom. Philosophy comes naturally to any sincere seeker

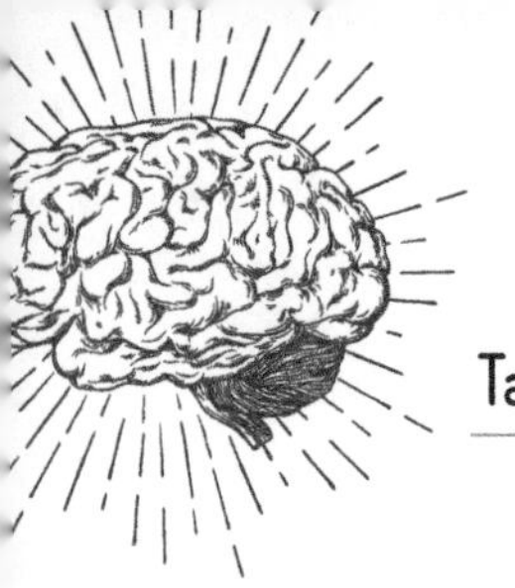

of truth. As the ancient Greek philosopher Plato said, "Philosophy begins in wonder." All students need to do is be themselves, express their ideas, and listen to the ideas of others.

JCU P4K interns are paid for their work by an endowment given to the JCU Department of Philosophy. However, our interns regularly insist that they would gladly do their work for free. I'll repeat that because I find it extraordinary: *Our interns, who work minimum wage jobs at local pizza joints to pay their expensive tuition, regularly tell me that they would gladly do their work at P4K for free.* I, in turn, insist that if the money weren't there I would simply arrange for interns to receive course credit for this valuable learning experience.

I'm telling you this to encourage you to start a P4K program at your school. Contact the philosophy department at your local college or university to ask if any undergraduates would be available to present or teach. Colleges and universities can often arrange funding or course credit through their career centers. This type of internship could also count as service learning for various programs and districts. Short of finding college interns, you can easily run your own philosophy classroom without any help. If undergraduates can do it without any special training, then so can you. Our interns often use the books *Philosophy for Teens* and *More Philosophy for Teens*, which I wrote with my colleague Paul Thomson 15 years ago for an earlier version of the P4K program. These books provide an accessible introduction to the entire history of philosophy.

Recently, as I listened to the kinds of discussions going on in our P4K classroom, I realized we needed another book more exclusively dedicated to contemporary controversial issues. *Take a Stand!* was designed and written by JCU's P4K interns. They generated the list of issues, researched both sides, and presented them in a format they know from experience works.

Each chapter begins with a dialogue between two fictional high school students. The dialogue shows how philosophical issues naturally arise in ordinary conversation. A nice way to start class is to ask two theatrical students to perform the dialogue. This allows for some giggles and direct engagement with the arguments to be examined.

Each chapter then examines the issue from each side, with the aim of displaying an unbiased balance. The authors have highlighted interesting and outspoken experts on the issues, explained their views, and summarized their arguments. As your students read these passages, they can consider which side they are on—whom they agree with more and why. This is critical thinking: analyzing an issue in order to form a judgment of their own.

Finally, the authors offer a personal statement on the issue. This section provides a concrete example of how one might apply the ideas presented in the chapter to one's own life. It makes the authors more real to the reader as role models. Discussion questions are included at the end of each chapter, along with a set of classroom activities that will enable students to work with the issues in a hands-on way.

I hope you enjoy using this book as much as we enjoyed creating it. I wish you many insightful philosophy discussions, both in class and beyond.

Introduction

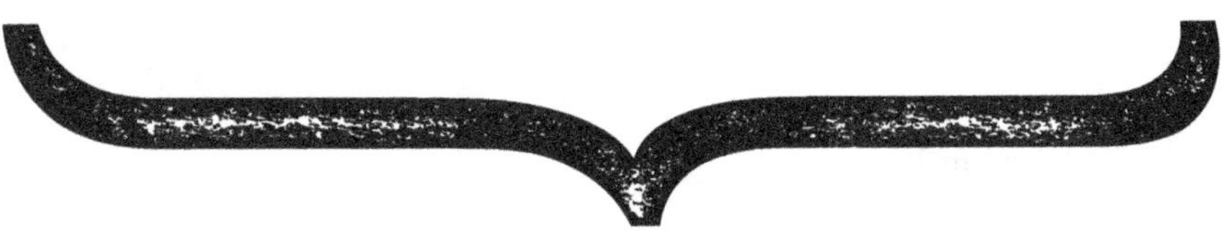

by Eric Johnston

Suppose I told you I can prove that cows don't eat. You would be unlikely to believe me. But what if I made an argument you can't resist? My argument takes just two steps. The first:

All animals either eat or are eaten.

Surely you accept this statement, as it is a basic principle of biology. Out in the wilderness, there are predators and prey. Survival of the fittest means organisms have to find food and avoid becoming the food of others, which leads to the second step:

Cows are animals that are eaten.

Hamburgers have to come from somewhere. Whether you personally like them or not, beef is a popular food.

So far, so good. Now put the two steps together—you get a surprising result:

1. All animals either eat or are eaten.
2. Cows are animals that are eaten.
3. *Therefore, cows do not eat.*

If you accept the first step and the second step, then you cannot escape this conclusion. After all, the first step argues that the entire set of animals can be divided into two groups, as shown in Diagram 1.

The second step states that cows are in the second group. The conclusion states that, because the two groups do not overlap, cows cannot be in the first group. What's going on here?

DOI: 10.4324/9781003238393-1

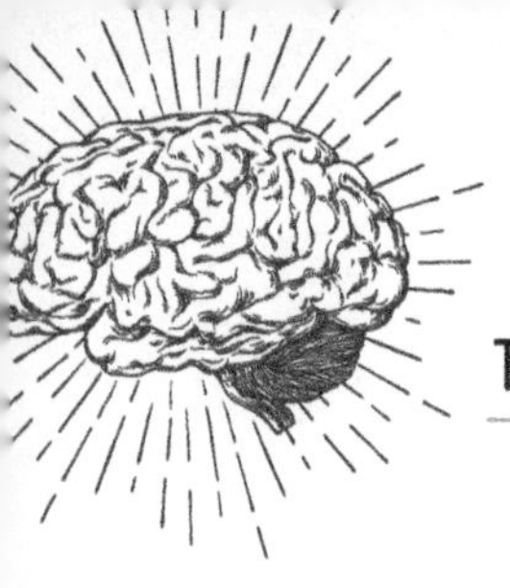

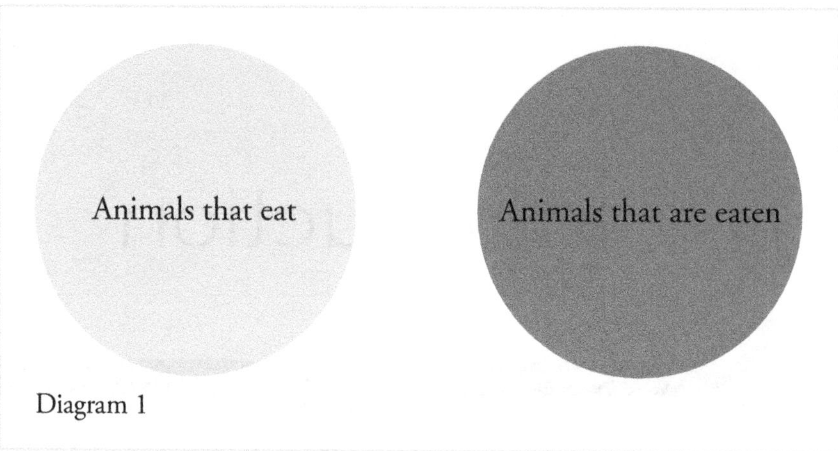

Diagram 1

This example is just a trick of logic. The first step of my argument is true in a *loose* sense—if you interpret it as meaning that animals can be categorized as predators or prey. But it is not true in a *strict* sense—if you interpret it as meaning that every animal either only eats or only is eaten. In fact, this strict sense is clearly false, because prey have to eat in order to fatten up enough to be prey. The trick was getting you to agree to the loose sense at first, and then using the strict sense later, within the argument.

Human beings are naturally logical, born with the ability to reason about how the world works—and this is what makes humans such a successful species. However, humans are also naturally prone to making logical mistakes. Especially when thinking about complex topics they feel passionate about, humans are easily tricked into drawing false conclusions.

A long time ago, a man named Socrates noticed this. He lived in Athens, Greece, which established the world's very first democracy. He was proud of his fellow Athenians for running such a sophisticated society, with lawyers, priests, artists, doctors, teachers, and so on, all playing their part. But he was also worried about them because, when he spoke to them in the marketplace, he found that they were not very good at defending their goals and values.

"What is justice?" he would ask the lawyers. The lawyers couldn't agree on an answer, and not one of them could make a decent argument. The same was true when he asked priests about holiness, artists about beauty, doctors about health, teachers about knowledge, and so on. None of the "experts" were experts after all.

Socrates worried that a democracy based on ignorance would soon fall apart. So, he set out to help his fellow Athenians improve their reasoning skills. Calling himself a philosopher, meaning "lover of wisdom," he spent his days talking to the youth of Athens about the logical mistakes of so-called experts. Unfortunately, this made the experts so angry that they had Socrates arrested for "corrupting the youth." Although he could have escaped, Socrates chose to accept the verdict against him, which was execution by poison.

But the attempt to stamp out philosophy backfired. Socrates's young followers set up a school where they could continue to practice the love of wisdom. Called the Academy, it was the first university in the world. There, philosophers reasoned about all sorts of com-

Depiction of the Death of Socrates

plex and passionate issues. They learned how to make good arguments for their views and how to criticize bad arguments in a constructive way. Philosophy became a permanent part of society, helping people to improve their reasoning skills beyond anything Socrates could have imagined. It helped democracy survive.

To this day, people continue to make logical mistakes, and philosophers continue to set them straight. There is a real difference between good and bad arguments. Some arguments can reliably move step-by-step to a true conclusion; others fail to make sense on close examination. Studying logic enables people to see the difference.

Three main logical concepts will be needed in order to sort through the controversial issues in this book: deductive validity, soundness, and logical fallacies.

Deductive Validity

A deductively valid argument is structured so that, if each of the supporting steps is true, then the conclusion *must* be true. For example:

1. All mice are mammals.
2. All mammals are animals.
3. Therefore, all mice are animals.

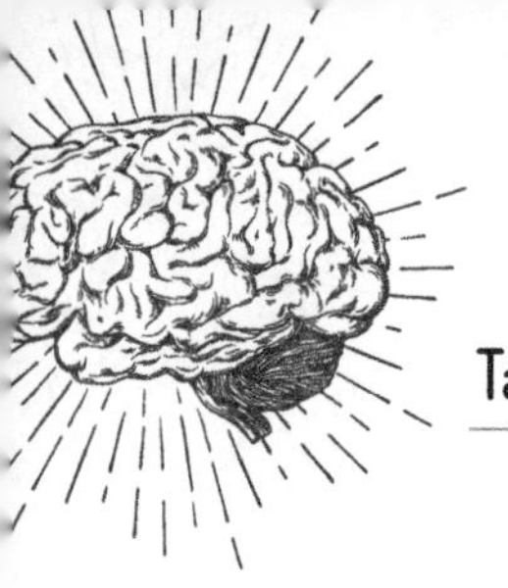

In a **deductively valid argument**, it is impossible for the premises to be true while the conclusion is false.

A diagram can be used to show how the steps necessitate the conclusion. The first step says that all mice are mammals, which can be represented in Diagram 2.

The second step says that all mammals are animals, which can be represented in Diagram 3.

Now put the two steps together, and you'll see that you cannot avoid the conclusion, as represented in Diagram 4.

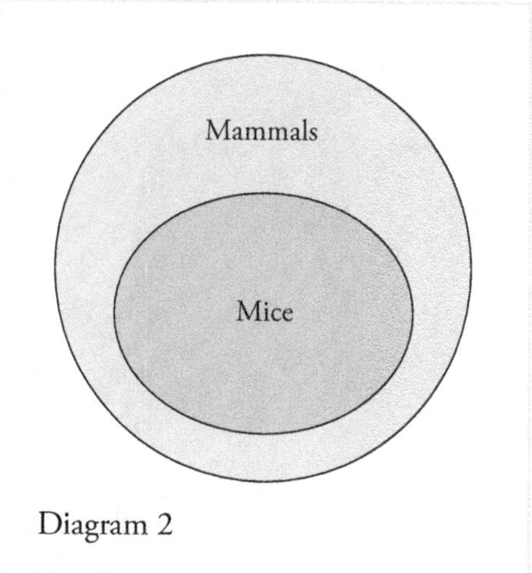

Diagram 2

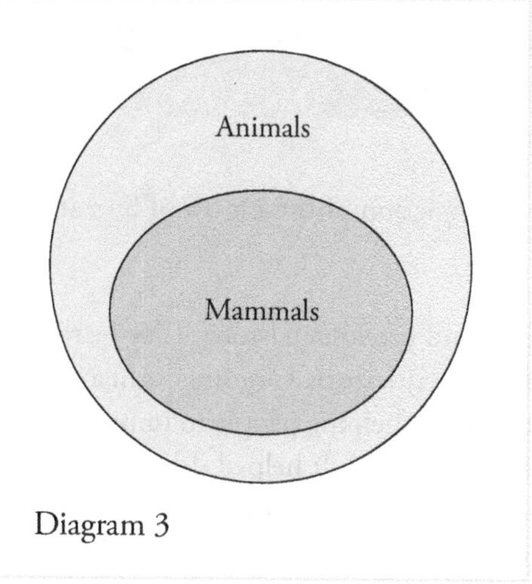

Diagram 3

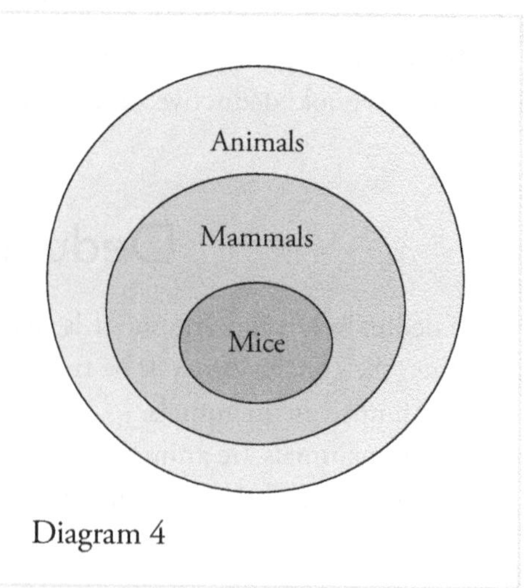

Diagram 4

In a deductively valid argument, the truth of the premises guarantees the truth of the conclusion. This is not just a matter of opinion. It is a fact—as objective as any mathematical fact, like 2 + 2 = 4. A good argument is like an equation: The inference from the steps to the conclusion is necessary.

However, deductive validity is not enough to make a good argument. This is evident in the following example:

1. All snakes are mammals.
2. All mammals are trees.
3. Therefore, all snakes are trees.

This argument is deductively valid. Go ahead and draw the diagram—it is exactly the same as the diagram drawn for mice. So, the inference is necessary: If you accept the steps, you *have to* accept the conclusion. But, of course, you should not accept the steps. They are both false.

Soundness

The second logical concept needed for evaluating arguments is soundness. For an argument to be sound, the steps must not only add up to the conclusion, but also correspond to reality. In the previous example, the steps about snakes and trees do not correspond to reality. So, even though the argu-

ment is deductively valid, it is not sound. In this instance, judging soundness seems just as objective as judging validity.

However, in most instances, judging soundness is subjective, meaning that it will vary from person to person. Take the following example:

1. All ducks fly.
2. Anything that flies is beautiful.
3. Therefore, all ducks are beautiful.

A **sound argument** is deductively valid, and all of its steps are actually true.

This argument is deductively valid, because the steps necessarily imply the conclusion. However, the second step is clearly a matter of opinion. Does that make it unsound?

Not necessarily. Suppose that I judge this argument to be sound, while you judge it unsound. Because there is no higher judge to decide who is right, we can simply agree to disagree. We might both marshal further reasons for our side of the debate. One of us might convince the other. But we may not be able to settle the matter, and that's okay. Soundness is a subjective judgement.

Although validity is a matter of fact, soundness is a matter of personal opinion. It is important to realize this when examining the arguments in this book. The chapter contributors examine both sides of a number of controversial issues. They are careful to construct a deductively valid argument for each side. But they cannot tell you which side's argument is sound. This is for you to decide.

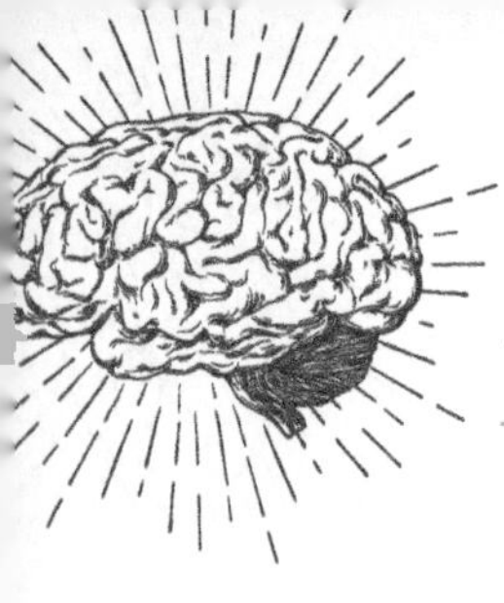

Logical Fallacies

Philosophers love to debate controversial issues. They work hard to construct arguments for their point of view. Over the years, they have discovered a number of surefire ways to go wrong, called logical fallacies. Logical fallacies are not always obvious, and even the best philosophers have fallen victim to them. The following are some of the most common logical fallacies found in arguments, along with real-world examples.

Hasty Generalization

This is when a person judges a statement to be true without sufficient evidence.

> **Zamir:** I went to Chipotle for the first time and experienced rude customer service. Chipotle is a terrible restaurant! I'm never going to any Chipotle again.

In this example, Zamir has one bad experience and, on that basis, infers that all of Chipotle's restaurants will reproduce that same bad experience. But note that a problem with one employee is not likely to affect the chain as a whole. Because the speaker gives no reason why it would, he is not justified in drawing such a general conclusion.

Ad Hominem

This is when a person attacks the character of the person who is advancing the argument rather than disproving the truth of their argument.

> **Ryan:** Are you really going to listen to your overweight doctor? She clearly doesn't have any idea of what's actually good for the body—only what's good for her taste buds!

In this example, Ryan is attacking and insulting the character of the doctor rather than trying to refute her methods of practicing medicine. In fact, an unhealthy person (or one who *appears* unhealthy) may be perfectly able to help others be healthy. The appearance of an individual need not affect their understanding of health, and so people should not let it bias their judgment.

Appeal to Irrelevant Authority

This is when a person supports a statement by appealing to someone who commands respect, just because they command respect.

> **Ja'maya:** It's finally settled. Bigfoot exists. The Governor of Massachusetts has announced it on television.

The Governor of Massachusetts may be an expert on state politics, but this expertise has nothing to do with legendary monsters. What he declares to be true about Bigfoot should not sway Ja'maya. Philosophers grant that some authorities are relevant. For example, a doctor can provide an expert opinion on a patient's health. Even in such a case, however, philosophers caution that authoritative statements never *guarantee* truth.

Post Hoc

This is when event A precedes event B, and a person concludes that event A must have caused event B.

> **Connor:** I always wear my lucky jersey when watching my favorite basketball team play. When I wore it last Tuesday, my team won. I forgot to wear it Thursday, and my team lost. The jersey must have been responsible in both cases.

A spectator wearing an article of clothing cannot influence the success of a sports team. Inevitably, the correlation will break down. Connor may ignore these instances or try to explain them away. People love to see a causal connection between things when there is only an accidental correlation. Perhaps this is because causality gives a stronger sense of understanding and control. This does not make it logical.

False Dilemma

This is when a person offers a short list of options and implies that there are no other options.

> **Russel:** Son, are you going to eat your broccoli? Either eat it now, or it goes to waste. It is your choice.

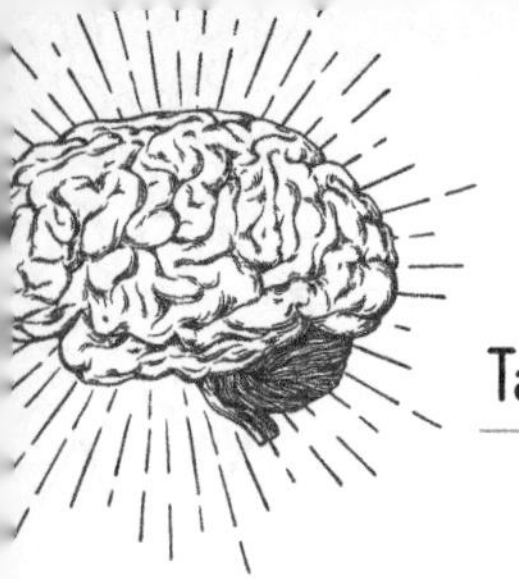

In this example, a father presents his son with only two possible choices when there are actually many more. The broccoli could be saved for later, given to another member of the family, composted, etc. The dilemma presented is not a fair representation of the situation.

Straw Man

This is when a person falsely attributes a lame argument to their critic while dismissing the actual argument.

> **Lidya:** It should be illegal to kill cats in city limits with a shotgun, especially for the purpose of sport.
> **Ryder:** Give me a break. It's absurd to think that everyone in the city is walking around with a shotgun shooting at cats.

Ryder is attacking the claim that a lot of people are shooting at cats. But this is not exactly the claim Lidya made. She was claiming that the law should forbid shooting cats even if there aren't that many people doing it.

Begging the Question

This is when a person assumes the very thing they are trying to prove.

> **Emmanuel:** I know you stole my bike, Devon, because you are such a thief.

Here Emmanuel is trying to prove Devon is a thief on the grounds that he is a thief. What Emmanuel needs to do instead is give some evidence or reason why he thinks Devon is a thief. Otherwise, he is really just using his conclusion as a step in his argument. Begging the question is also called *circular reasoning*.

Personal Statement

The study of philosophy has always been an important part of my life, all of the way through my college studies. I took my first philosophy course as a sophomore in college and was introduced to the subject as a formal field of study. Even before I took my first class, every thought and belief I held inevitably fell under the scrutiny of logic and philosophy. Furthermore, every thought and belief has ultimately been *improved* by philosophy. My friendships, morality, and pursuit of happiness have all been formed from my attempts to apply and understand philosophical wisdom. It is not always possible to find answers—

never mind simple answers—to the most intriguing questions about existence. However, philosophy has been my personal journey for pursuing these answers.

Discussion Questions

1. What do you think about the charge against Socrates? Does encouraging young people to ask questions and argue issues corrupt them?
2. Construct a deductively valid argument about the topic of your choice.
3. Can you think of an instance when someone has used a logical fallacy to convince you of something? If so, what was the argument, and which fallacy did they use?
4. What is the difference between a valid argument and a sound argument?
5. What is the goal of deductive reasoning?

Classroom Activities

1. Find three examples of logical fallacies people have actually committed on Twitter.
2. Play the classic board game Clue. Write down your reasoning for your conclusion about who the killer is in the form of a deductively valid argument. (Search for "deductively valid argument forms" for some helpful patterns to use.)

References

Dowden, B. (n.d.). *Fallacies*. Internet Encyclopedia of Philosophy. https://www.iep.utm.edu/fallacy

Internet Encyclopedia of Philosophy. (n.d.). *Validity and soundness*. https://www.iep.utm.edu/val-snd

Nails, D. (2018). Socrates. In E. N. Zalta (Ed.), *Stanford encyclopedia of philosophy* (Spring 2020 ed.). https://plato.stanford.edu/entries/socrates

PART 1
TECHNOLOGY

Chapter 1

Are Video Games a Waste of Time?

by
Rachel C. Lee

[Annie rings Sean's doorbell and asks him to join her on a bike ride.]

Sean: Why don't you come inside instead and check out this new video game I got!

Annie: *[Glancing into the house at the television screen]* Oh, *that* game. My brother has been playing that. It's a waste of time.

Sean: What do you mean? I played last night, and it was loads of fun.

Annie: Yeah, maybe it is, but my brother plays it for about 5 hours a day. He's like a zombie, just pressing buttons and staring at the screen.

Sean: I'll admit it's easy to get hooked on video games. But it's okay with this one because it has a great story.

Annie: Well, I can see how video games might be okay for kids learning how to read, or type, or build simulations. But otherwise they're just a waste of time.

Sean: Something's not a waste of time if you enjoy it. Is it a waste of time to look at a painting in an art museum?

Annie: Of course not. Great paintings inspire people in so many ways.

DOI: 10.4324/9781003238393-3

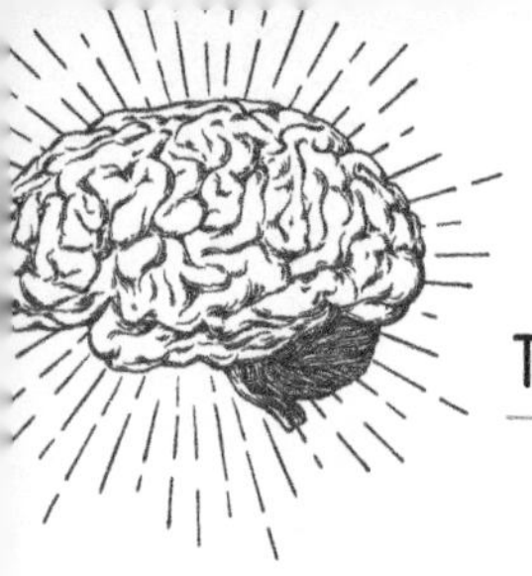

Sean: Exactly, and playing a great video game isn't any different from enjoying great art.

Annie: Games aren't the same as art at all. They're competitive. You spend all of your time trying to outdo other people.

Sean: First of all, what's wrong with competition? Do you blame Olympic gold medalists for spending all of their time trying to outdo other people? Second, not all games are competitive. In some, you build cool things, sometimes with other people.

Annie: Olympic gold medalists, artists, and carpenters get a lot more fresh air and exercise than button mashers do.

Sean: I grant that everyone needs some fresh air and exercise. But a lot of professions require grown adults to sit at computer monitors for 8 hours a day. It's hypocritical to say that's okay for adults but not for kids.

Annie: All I know is that I'm glad I have other hobbies. See you around.

Art: A form of creative expression, produced and appreciated by humans for its beauty and emotional power.

Competition: An activity in which people work against one another to gain something.

Video games are generally adored by young people and disliked by parents. Whether the game of choice is a multiplayer shooter or a single-player platformer, it can absorb its players for hours on end and become a distraction from real-life affairs. Many scientific articles have criticized video games for their influence on the developing minds of young people, while countless bloggers and game reviewers argue that video games are thought-provoking, mentally enriching, and even an art form in themselves.

So how should people regard video games? Are they a waste of time, or can they lead people to think deeply—even philosophically—in ways that they haven't before? Many 21st-century thinkers have tried to answer these questions.

Aaron Smuts argued that art has many definitions and can take many forms; video games would count as an art form based on most of these definitions. He also pointed out that museums have begun including video games in their more contemporary, interactive exhibits. Smuts admitted that not all video games should count as art. In particular, he maintained that some games are competitive in nature, which makes them pastimes, in his view, rather than art.

Anyone who has played a single-player adventure game knows that not all video games promote competition. Some have a focus on storytelling and providing a sensory experience for the player. Smuts pointed to the increasing visual detail of video games as proof of artistic merit. Developers are also putting more and more effort into the accompanying music. Smuts believed video games can be considered art even though they are competitive. After all, poems and other art forms can be created for the purpose of competition without undermining their artistic nature.

Smuts's Argument FOR Video Games

1. Some video games are art.
2. Appreciating art is a valuable experience.
3. Playing a video game is a way of appreciating it.
4. Therefore, playing some video games is a valuable experience.

Gambling: Playing a game of chance, typically one that involves betting money.

However, it's possible that video games could still be a waste of time if their value as art is being ignored. The competitive nature of a video game could absorb the players' attention, distracting them from the beauty that makes the game art. People typically play a game for hours upon hours because they enjoy the competition. If this kind of competition is a waste of time, then playing wouldn't be the same as appreciating art. For example, have you ever enjoyed the way a game looks or found yourself interested by its story, only to forget about these things once you begin competing for the fastest time or the most victories?

But distraction is not the only problem with competition. Jeffrey Barlow showed how the competitive nature of video games could promote gambling and even normalize violence. Barlow explained that when people compete against each other online, they can motivate one another to spend unhealthy amounts of time playing. They are missing out on fresh air, sunshine, and physical human contact. Some players end up losing sleep, eating poorly, and even dying as an effect of their unhealthy interest in continuing to play video games.

Moreover, the world of gaming offers many opportunities for attaching monetary value to winning—but this is gambling. Kids lack sufficient understanding of personal

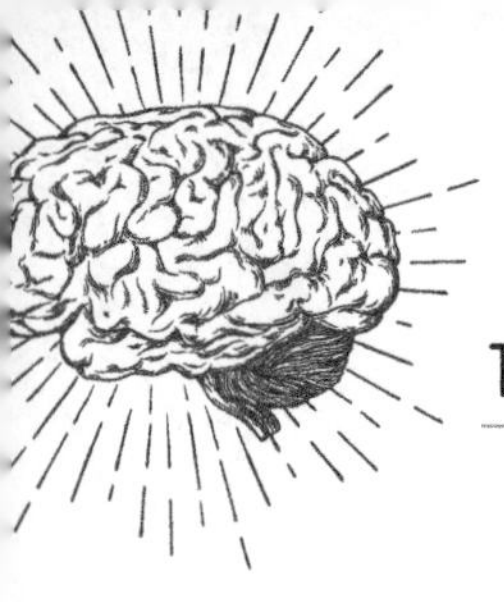

finances to be responsible gamblers. They also might begin to expect a prize for everything they do, which is not a very realistic approach to life.

Finally, the violence included in games might affect players' behavior in a variety of ways. Barlow specifically mentioned that *Doom*, a popular video game, was connected to the first high school shooting in the United States. Repeatedly engaging in violence during gaming can normalize violence for the player, making it more likely for them to be violent in real life.

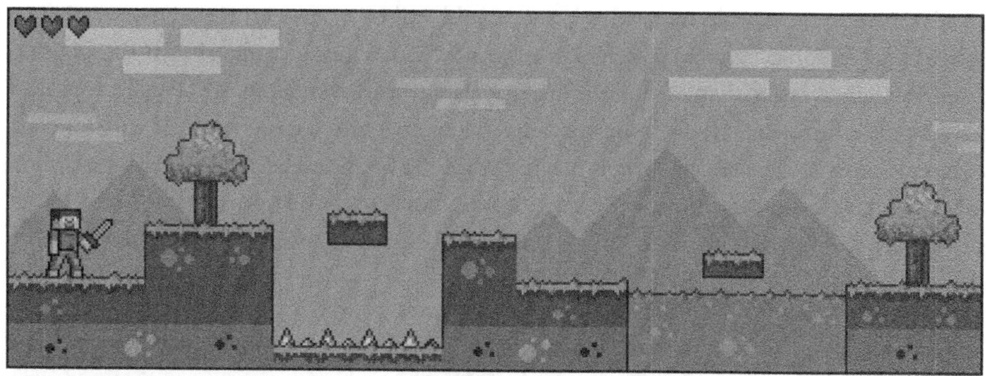

Barlow's Argument *AGAINST* Video Games

1. Most video games are competitive.
2. Competition could lead to an obsessive interest in the game.
3. Obsessive interests are not healthy.
4. Therefore, most video games are not healthy pastimes.

Interestingly, kids' sports are also very competitive. Suppose Joe is so determined to win the state basketball championship that he practices day after day for hours on end. He does the same repetitive drills alone under fluorescent lights at the gym. He loses friends and falls behind in his academic subjects. He grabs fast food for dinner and drinks a lot of Gatorade. He takes his team to the championship. Does Joe have an obsessive interest in basketball? Where does the line fall between a healthy passion and an unhealthy one? If Joe's passion was for competitive gaming instead of basketball, would his behavior be any more or less healthy?

The 19th-century philosopher John Stuart Mill can help frame questions about video games. Mill famously introduced a distinction between higher pleasures and lower pleasures. Higher pleasures improve people's overall happiness by activating "higher faculties"—they make people behave in ways that only humans behave. For example, a stirring documentary might motivate you to debate a controversial issue with friends. Lower pleasures, although appealing in the short term, ultimately make people unhappier. For example, watching a silly cartoon for 2 hours won't motivate you to do anything. In fact, it

might make you feel depressed about falling behind on the homework you were supposed to be doing!

Think of a video game you or a friend has played recently. Did the game activate any higher faculties by raising and examining a controversial issue? Did it teach complex information to the player? Did it promote social bonding and problem solving? Or did the game appeal to lower pleasures, such as procrastination? Or was it a mix of both? You may have to analyze the content of each particular game to determine whether and to what extent it is a waste of time.

Personal Statement

I developed a passion for video games at a young age. Like most kids, my fascination with games had to do with their sensory appeal—the bright colors and weird sounds that poured from the screen. As I grew older, I also learned from games. I learned how to stay focused in chaotic environments while playing first-person shooters, and I even picked up important vocabulary from role-playing games. These skills could have been learned in a more academic environment, but I also found value and joy in learning this way because the games themselves were a joy for me.

If I ask myself whether all of my hours spent playing video games could have been spent working toward a greater goal, such as publishing a book, I know that video games were arguably a waste of time. Still, I consider how video games motivated me to make up my own stories and eventually to write them down. I believe the inspiration that I received from gaming made me a more creative person. Without those hours in front of a screen, would I be the avid writer that I am today?

Like many other activities, gaming could be a waste of time if the player is simply using the video game as an escape from their responsibilities or boredom. If the player chooses to experience the game as they would experience a poem or painting, then they might have a more enriching experience.

Discussion Questions

1. Think of your favorite video game, or a friend's. Do you consider it art? Why or why not?
2. Think of an avid gamer you know. Do you think that their interest in games might be unhealthy? Why or why not?
3. Is there a quality (or set of qualities) that distinguishes an artistic game from a game that might be a waste of time?
4. How long is too long to be playing a game? What criteria would you use to determine a healthy time limit?
5. What do you think about Mill's distinction between higher and lower pleasures? Is there an objective way to rate pleasures, or is it all just a matter of opinion?

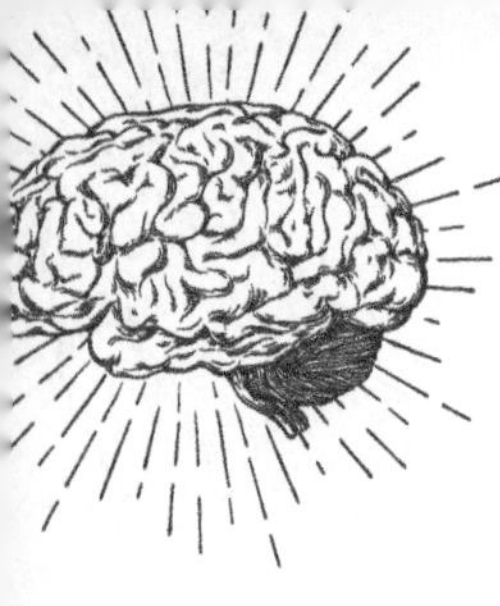

Classroom Activities

1. Make a painting or drawing of video game worlds you would like to create. Share them with a classmate and discuss the unique features of your game worlds.
2. Make a chart showing how much time you spend playing video games versus engaging in physical exercise in a given week. Share your charts and discuss ideal time ratios.

References

Barlow, J. (2003). Upon the importance (and dangers) of playing video games. *Interface: The Journal of Education, Community and Values, 3*(7).

Kroll, J. (2000). *'Emotion engine'? I don't think so.* Newsweek. https://www.newsweek.com/emotion-engine-i-dont-think-so-156675

Smuts, A. (2005). Are video games art? *Contemporary Aesthetics, 3*(1). https://digitalcommons.risd.edu/liberalarts_contempaesthetics/vol3/iss1/6

Chapter 2

Is It Rude to Text in Class?

by
Eric Johnston

[Charles and Buck enter math class and sit down at their desks.]

Charles: Buck! Class is starting. Put away your phone, or the teacher will take it!

Buck: I'll be fine—the school approved classroom electronic devices at the beginning of the year.

Charles: I know, but you're only supposed to use electronics for good reasons. It's rude to sit in class and randomly text your friends.

Buck: It's my phone. It's my education at stake. I should have the right to free speech, which includes texting whoever I want. So I'm not doing anything outside of my rights. Why would I want to conform my actions to what other people think is polite?

Charles: I guess it's true that you have the right to be rude. But you can't live your life like that. I mean, you have the right to lie to me, but I would still be mad. You have to respect people. It's the only way we can all get along and understand one another.

Buck: I'm not sure why you think the problem is on me. I mean, I think it's rude that the teacher expects me to act against my best interests to appease

DOI: 10.4324/9781003238393-4

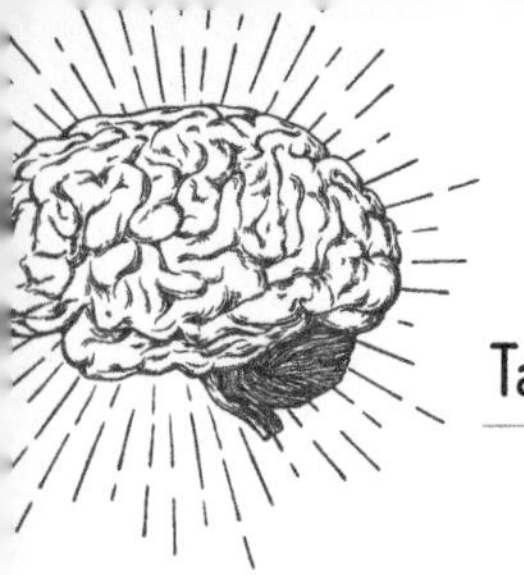

her. That sounds pretty imposing and ignorant to me. What does it even mean to say something is rude?

Manners: Social customs and rituals that people use to express moral attitudes, commitments, and character.

Charles: Well, something that's rude upsets other people because it shows disregard for their well-being. Being polite is a way of cooperating with the people around us.

Buck: It seems like your view leaves it open for anyone to define what counts as rude. Each person is likely to differ in their requirements for well-being depending on their beliefs and culture. Even if I wanted to be polite, I would never know how to uniquely appease each person. Last, and most importantly: What about *me*? What about *my* well-being?

Charles: Buck! I can't believe you're so selfish.

Buck: I can't believe you're so obedient.

Teacher: Buck! Charles! If you two don't be quiet, I will have to send you to the principal's office. This is a learning environment. Now zip it! You're being rude!

As smartphones grow ever smarter, texting in class is becoming a matter of increasing conflict between students and teachers. Upon first glance, it seems to be a trivial matter of school policy. On closer examination, however, this issue raises a number of large questions that evade simple answers. This chapter examines the central concepts at stake, so you will be able to draw an educated conclusion about texting in the classroom.

As the dialogue illustrates, teachers tend to regard texting as rude, while students regard it as their right. So, first of all, what exactly is rudeness? Rudeness is a violation of polite behavior. It's not a *crime*, because it's not a violation of the law. Nor is it quite *immoral*, because it's not a violation of morality. Still, it is a violation of a code known in human society as politeness or manners.

Behaving politely is not confined to a narrow set of behaviors such as saying "please" and "thank you." Politeness is a large network of different beliefs and attitudes about thousands of different actions in thousands of situations. For example, recently, when I was walking my dog, he peed on my neighbor's garbage can, which was sitting by the road. Was it rude of me to allow that? Because every day brings new situations, it is impossible to create a complete list of manners. So how do people have any idea of how to judge whether an action is rude?

People learn manners through experience and observation, specifically observing how those around them act and react to what they do. It is easy to imagine how one might come to a completely different understanding of manners by simply spending time around different people. Children who are raised with different parents, attend different schools, or are a part of different socioeconomic classes will all have unique influences as they grow up that could reward different rituals or customs. For example, I have a Muslim neighbor whose family regards dogs as unclean. I try to keep my dog away from their yard altogether.

Every human culture around the world has some concept of manners, but the philosopher's job is to think critically about the facts. Are manners a good thing? What is the purpose of manners, and should people be concerned about preserving them? Karen Stohr, an ethicist, argued that people should. In her view, manners are more significant than a regurgitation of surrounding behavior. They are communication devices through which people express their social intentions. By conforming to the expected behavior, people communicate a willingness to cooperate with one another and form a healthy community.

This is not to say that all manners are of equal significance. Stohr acknowledged that one can know what fork to use for the salad and still possess a "rotten" character. But using the right fork is one small clue among many that helps build a picture of what a person is really like. Someone who automatically opens the door for others and expresses congratulations for others' victories and condolences for their grief—even when those others are strangers—demonstrates that they are not self-centered, but committed to the well-being of society as a whole.

Stohr maintained that, in a healthy community, everyone has to be on equal footing. If one person regards themselves as more important than the others, cooperation breaks down, ultimately leaving people unable to accomplish joint ventures. Manners help to prevent this from happening. Stohr wrote:

> When I join a line by going to the end of it, I signal to the other people waiting that I intend to abide by the established conventions regarding lines. My expressed willingness to adhere to the convention communicates my belief that I stand on an equal footing with them, that I don't regard my needs and priorities as more important than theirs just because they happen to be mine.

Keeping society running smoothly is a joint venture. Like all joint ventures, it requires self-sacrifice. Tiny acts of politeness demonstrate that people are capable of cooperation, not solely interested in themselves.

Although Stohr did not directly address texting in class, her analysis can easily be applied to this case. She might argue that students should not text in class because it communicates that they regard their own needs and priorities as most important.

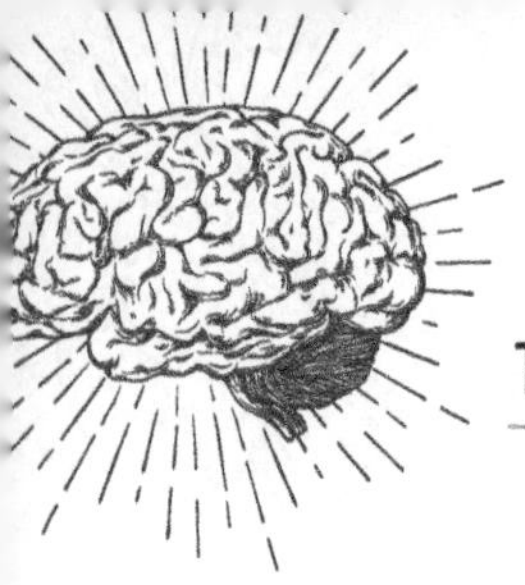

A Stohrian Argument *AGAINST* Texting

1. Texting in the classroom is selfish.
2. Selfishness destroys cooperation.
3. Destroying cooperation is rude.
4. Therefore, texting in the classroom is rude.

A **right** is automatic, official permission to do something.

If everyone agreed that it was rude to use their cell phone in the classroom, then it would rarely occur. For example, everyone agrees that it is rude to fart in an elevator. Therefore, it rarely occurs, and when it does, the perpetrator is embarrassed and apologetic. The problem with using cell phones in the classroom is that *teachers* typically consider this rude, while *students* typically don't.

Many students would agree that selfishness destroys cooperation and that destroying cooperation in the classroom is rude. Therefore, perhaps they simply don't see texting as selfish. Does the current student generation have a new standard of behavior that allows for more individualistic activity, which the current teacher generation views as selfish? If so, which standard should prevail?

Teachers often claim that they have the right to set the standard in their classroom. But what if the students view the classroom as theirs? Shouldn't they then have the right to set the standard? After all, every new generation rejects much of what the old generation has left behind. The technology, fashion, and music of one's parents become obsolete. Why should students agree to live by teachers' manners?

Scottish philosopher and educator A. S. Neill regarded most politeness as harmful conformity. Maybe teachers do consider it rude to text in class, but for Neill, that alone isn't a good enough reason to expect students to stop. Neill found that freedom from peer pressure and authority was much more important than conformity to social customs. This is not because he thought there is no value in cooperation, but because he thought true cooperation must be freely chosen by the individuals involved.

In 1921 Neill founded an experimental school called Summerhill, the world's first "children's democracy" where attendance was not required, there were no tests, and the students made all of the rules. Not surprisingly, those lucky students loved school, and Summerhill is still going strong a century later (see http://www.summerhillschool.co.uk).

At Summerhill, Neill made the observation that, although kids who are raised under strict authoritarian influences *act* politely, they are only doing so out of fear, and their manners are insincere and phony. He thought the reason *why* a student acts politely is just as important, if not more important, than the act of politeness itself. For example, would it really be polite if someone put their phone away in class only because they thought the teacher might take it away? Of course not! The student is not really trying to cooperate with the teacher; the student is just acting in fear of consequences.

Aside from freedom being critical to truly sincere politeness, Neill also argued that freedom is crucial to a child's development, especially in the classroom, and any act of

authority against a child is actually wrong. True development, motivation, and discovery must come from self-interest, not fear. Neill wrote:

> You cannot make children learn music or anything else without to some degree converting them into will-less adults. You fashion them into accepters of the status-quo—a good thing for a society that needs obedient sitters at dreary desks, standers in shops, mechanical catchers of the 8:30 suburban train—a society, in short, that is carried on the shabby shoulders of the scared little man—the scared-to-death conformist.

When kids are deprived of their freedoms in the classroom, they are deprived of their ability to explore for themselves and act on self-interest, which is the most important experience a child can be given in school. The cost of imposing restrictions on kids' rights in the classroom is the cost of disturbing their discovery of truth.

A Neillian Argument *FOR* Texting

1. The only way to prevent texting in the classroom is through authoritative command.
2. Authoritative command replaces a student's self-interest with fear.
3. Replacing self-interest with fear prevents true learning.
4. It is wrong to prevent true learning in the classroom.
5. Therefore, it is wrong to prevent texting in the classroom through authoritative command.

Personal Statement

There isn't one objective answer to the question, "Is it rude to text in class?" Therefore, there is more than one legitimate way to answer the question. With each situation comes a different expectation from the audience, which means a different perception of manners. The ultimate decision to act either politely or rudely is a personal one. No matter your decision, it is important to understand the workings of the issue before you take a stance.

Discussion Questions

1. Do you think it is rude for your friends to text when you are trying to talk to them at lunch? How is this the same or different from the classroom situation?
2. Is texting equally rude in all company? For example, is it rude to text in front of friends, strangers, teachers, and family equally?

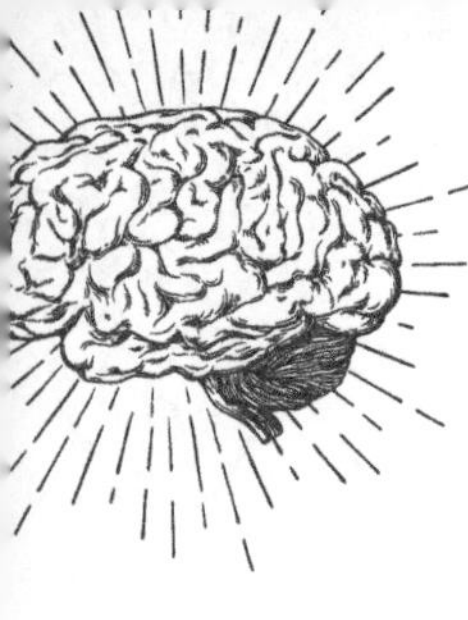

Discussion Questions, *continued*

3. What would be the outcome in society if everyone stopped caring about manners?
4. Are there times where it might be good to act rudely?
5. Would society be better if there was a law that required citizens to be polite?

Classroom Activities

1. Make your classroom into a democracy for a day. Have a meeting, propose activities and rules, and then vote on them. Everyone in the room, including the teacher, gets one equal vote.
2. Write and share stories about a world in which there are no manners. What happens there? Would you want to live there?

References

Neill, A. S. (1960). *Summerhill: A radical approach to child rearing.* Hart Publishing.
Stohr, K. (2012). *On manners.* Routledge.

Chapter 3

Should Parents Limit Kids' Screen Time?

[Naomi gets on the bus to school and sits down next to Lawrence.]

Naomi: Sorry I couldn't message you last night. My parents made me stay offline yesterday.

Lawrence: About time!

Naomi: What? Whose side are you on?

Lawrence: I just think you really need to detox. Did you have fun doing other stuff?

Naomi: Ugh, no! It's so boring at home without my phone and laptop. Plus, my parents don't understand how important it is for me to have Internet access. I have to keep track of my homework and emails on there.

Lawrence: But isn't it nice to disconnect sometimes? When my parents ask me to put my phone down, usually it's if they have something important to tell me, or if we're going to do something fun. In which case, I don't really mind.

Naomi: Are you kidding? You're okay with letting your parents control what you do with your phone? I don't think adults have any business restricting our screen time. Our phones are our window to the world.

 DOI: 10.4324/9781003238393-5

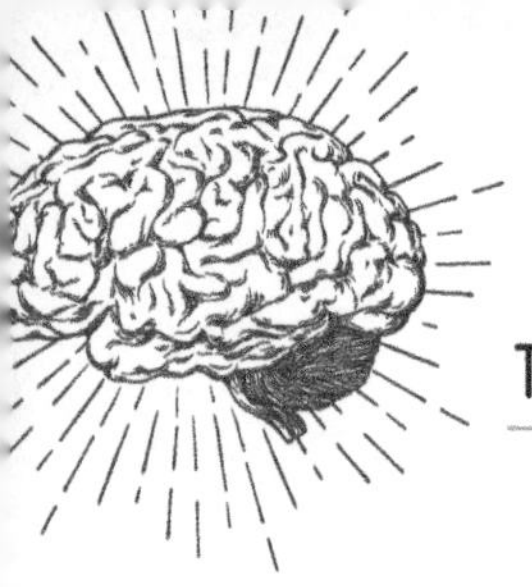

According to MedlinePlus, children under age 2 should have **no screen time**, and children over age 2 should be limited to **1–2 hours per day**.

Lawrence: Sure, technology is important for everyone. But don't you get sick of it sometimes? I get sucked into my phone some days, and it helps to be reminded that there's more to do with my life. When I'm online too much, I get kind of anxious. I feel isolated, even if I'm talking to friends on there, you know?

Naomi: I guess I can understand that. It's not like I want to be on my phone 24 hours a day. Still, if my parents really cared about me, maybe they would try to see why it's so important for me to be online.

Lawrence: My parents don't have much interest in anything to do with phones or computers. I think it's because they value real interaction much more. They want me to spend more time outside or in person with friends and family because that's what they think is more important.

Naomi: Well, I think screen time also counts as "real interaction." If my parents bothered to share that time with me, maybe they would realize it's not so bad.

Lawrence: Maybe you're right, but I still think my parents are just trying to look out for me.

Screen time refers to experiences with TV, computers, phones, and other devices. Today, many young people are constantly using screens to communicate with friends, watch their favorite shows, or play their favorite video games. In the past, screen time was limited to only a few devices (such as TVs and desktop computers). Now that young people have so many sources of screen time, their parents have felt the need to set limits. After all, spending almost every waking moment staring at a screen is bound to have consequences, such as a decrease in face-to-face social activity. This chapter will question whether parents should be limiting the amount and type of screen time their kids have.

Holly Hamilton-Bleakley, a contemporary philosophy professor, wrote about her son's interest in computer games. She noticed that although she and her family live in a neighborhood with plenty of other boys her son's age, none of these boys spend time with each other. Their parents jointly concluded that the boys' exposure to devices, such as computers and phones, had ruined their interest in spending time with one another face-to-face.

Hamilton-Bleakley aspired to change her son's behavior, allying with the other concerned parents in her neighborhood. She wanted to see her son sharing in-person experiences with the other boys. She cited the ancient Greek philosopher Aristotle to explain her reasoning: Living with other members of society allows people to develop their emotional intelligence and other valuable people skills.

Socialization: The activity of mixing socially with others; the process of learning to behave in a way that is acceptable to society.

However, if today's kids live in an increasingly digital world, maybe time spent online is teaching them exactly the social skills that they might need in adulthood. Suppose that kids spend all of their time away from screens, as their parents wish, only to be thrown into a workplace that relies heavily on communicating with that technology. How would they be better equipped than kids who had grown up practicing communication via screens? It is possible that parents such as Hamilton-Bleakley are speaking from a place of bias, simply because they grew up in a time when screens were not so integrated into many major aspects of daily life?

Hamilton-Bleakley went on to argue that by using screens excessively, kids are deprived of face-to-face socialization opportunities that might be right in front of them. Consider a child visiting their relative for the first time in years. If a tablet or phone is constantly within arm's reach, chances are the child will indulge in more screen time and might miss an important opportunity to socialize face-to-face.

In order for a young person to grow up with a healthy understanding of social interaction, they must first socialize with other people in their environment, learning from interpersonal experiences. Some online social skills might be useful, but overall, philosophers such as Hamilton-Bleakley believe that too much screen time will inevitably deprive kids of the socialization they need most.

Have you ever neglected an in-person social experience in favor of screen time? Do you think that parents should keep their kids from "missing out" on in-person socialization by setting strict limits on screen time? Or do you think kids themselves must be responsible for learning from the mistakes they might make with their devices?

Hamilton-Bleakley's Argument *FOR* Limits

1. Parents need to promote what is healthy and limit what is unhealthy for their kids.
2. Face-to-face interaction is healthy for kids.
3. Excessive screen time (more than 2 hours per day) is unhealthy for kids.
4. Therefore, parents need to promote face-to-face interaction and limit screen time for their kids.

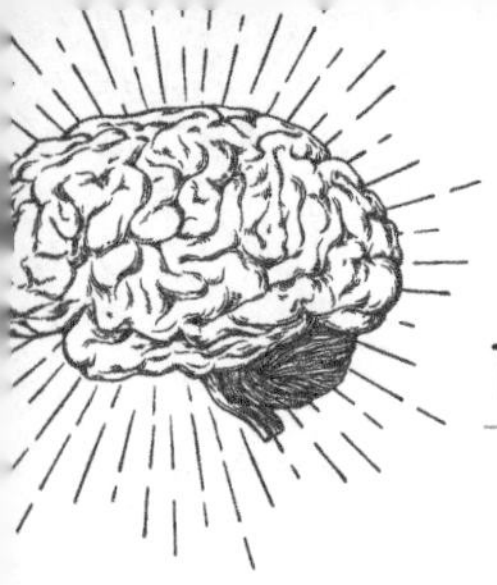

Other philosophers of the digital age believe that simply restricting screen time and forcing kids to interact in person is not the answer. Instead, as philosophy professor Jordan Shapiro argued, parents should strive to understand how their kids are spending their screen time and to spend that time *with* their kids, both to form family bonds and to supervise kids' online behavior. Instead of leaving a child to play their favorite video game alone in their room, Shapiro encouraged parents to pick up a second controller and experience the game alongside the child. Leading by example, Shapiro took steps to integrate screen time into many of his interactions with his kids. Dinnertime conversations in his household often include quick Google searches or a YouTube video. Shapiro emphasized that these experiences with his kids are not hindered by the presence of screens, but enhanced by them, because he has taken the time to understand why his kids value their devices.

Twenty-first-century life requires many people to stay connected with one another through technology, much of which involves screens. Most people would rather rely on technology for social interaction than focus solely on in-person experiences. Still, screen time can become a slippery slope that leads people away from social interaction, and kids are especially susceptible to misjudging the amount of time they spend with nothing but digital stimulation.

Shapiro further argued that kids should be allowed to explore social media even earlier than they already do. The sooner a child is exposed to screen time—moderated by a parent, of course—the better prepared they will be for a life of screens and digital connection.

Shapiro's Argument *AGAINST* Limits

1. Parents should encourage and guide kids in important aspects of today's culture.
2. Limiting something neither encourages it nor guides it.
3. Screen time is an important aspect of today's culture.
4. Therefore, parents should encourage and guide, not limit, kids' screen time.

Do you wish your parent would have spent more time enjoying video games or TV shows with you as a child, rather than telling you to turn them off? Would their guidance have helped you prepare for experiences with technology later in life? Or do you think that this involvement would have discouraged you from the activities that Hamilton-Bleakley valued, such as finding neighborhood friends and spending time outdoors?

Growing up, I witnessed my father's frustration at working in a field that he couldn't always relate to. He didn't give up on past difficult jobs because he wanted to provide a stable life for my whole family. Whether or not those experiences are more valuable than the ones he would have had in front of a screen is completely up for debate.

Thought Experiment

Consider an alternate universe in which you never accessed the Internet or looked at a screen of any sort. This means no news networks, funny videos, gaming, or instant messaging. What do you think you would have done with all of the time that would have been spent on screens? Would you be happier with how your time was spent, or would you have missed out? If your peers still had access to their devices in this scenario, do you think they would have accomplished more or had better life experiences than you? Would they now be more prepared for their future?

Personal Statement

Without siblings and with only a few close friends, I consider the Internet a heavy influence on my childhood. It was my pipeline of endless news, pop culture, funny videos, sad stories, and eventually, online friends. My parents, like many others, lived in total

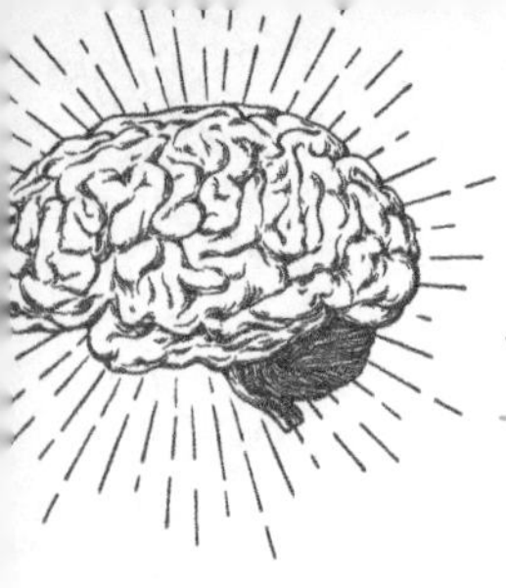

oblivion of my Internet escapades, warning me against sharing my personal information but otherwise leaving me to my own devices on unrestricted computers. I was one of countless kids who were handed the entire online world on a silver platter, free to browse the same conglomeration that hosts crime and ruins reputations on a daily basis.

I felt compelled to navigate this digital Wild West out of sheer curiosity, while also trying to succeed in school and bond with neighborhood friends as any child would. Finding a balance was difficult sometimes, and I remember many nights spent "studying" in my room when I was actually browsing my new favorite vlogging channel or messaging a friend across the country.

The Internet always excited me; on some days, it was the reason I got out of bed, thrilled to see if the creative fiction I had posted the night before had gained any followers or reviews. On other days, the excitement wasn't so positive. As a child, I suffered through anxious phases stemming from my first embarrassing blog post, my first computer virus, my first death threat from an angry stranger, and many other uncomfortable milestones in my online experience. I doubt I was the only child who was kept awake and sweating late at night due to these anxieties, which is why I personally believe that parents should be as involved as possible in their kids' online lives, restricting screen time when necessary.

Because I'm not currently a parent, I can't say exactly how I would raise my kids from birth to adulthood in regard to the Internet. However, I predict that I would place heavy restrictions on websites and talk regularly with my child about their experiences online. Considering current technological trends, I think that attempting to "ban" Internet access would do more harm than good in preparing any child for the life they're going to live. After all, kids need to learn how to seek jobs and stay in touch with friends or coworkers through their devices. Still, I believe that guiding my child away from any unnecessary sites would save them the worries and distress that so many people in my generation have struggled with.

Discussion Questions

1. Think of a time when using a device has been helpful, and think of a time when it was harmful. Do you think that screen time is worth the trouble it might cause?
2. Would you be willing to spend a week without looking at any screens whatsoever? What about a month? Do you think that your personal responsibilities would make this challenge impossible? If the challenge were possible, do you think the benefits of your time without screens might outweigh the drawbacks, even if you had to miss your favorite show or ignore your friends' messages?
3. Based on your own experiences with technology, if you were a parent, would you want to spend screen time with your child, discourage your child from having too much screen time, or try to find some balance of the two?

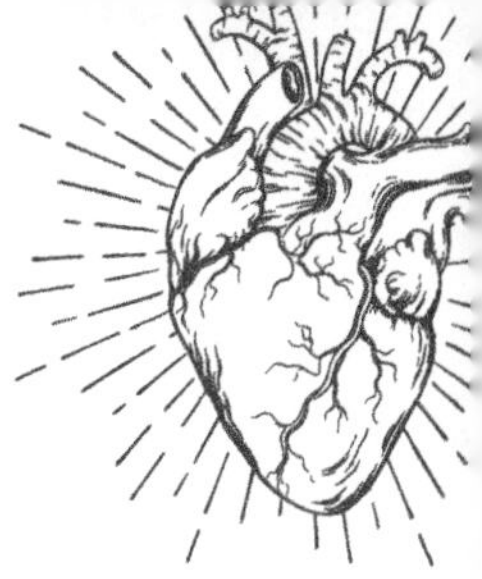

Discussion Questions, *continued*

4. If you had to advise a parent whose child was spending too much time on their devices, what would you tell the parent?
5. What do you think about face-to-face interaction? Is it important or overrated?

Classroom Activities

1. Estimate how much screen time you have had over the past year (you can base your calculation on a weekly average). Imagine you had spent that same amount of time learning an instrument or a language instead. If you could choose either past right now, which would you choose, and why? Share your answers.
2. Watch and discuss the 2016 documentary *Screenagers*.

References

Hamilton-Bleakley, H. (n.d.). *Summer notice: Your child is a social animal, not a virtual one.* Philosophy for Parents. https://philosophyforparents.com/tag/screen-time

Kamenetz, A. (2019). *Forget screen time rules—Lean in to parenting your wired child, author says.* NPR. https://www.npr.org/2019/01/15/679304393/forget-screen-time-rules-lean-in-to-parenting-your-wired-child

MedlinePlus. (2019). *Screen time and children.* https://medlineplus.gov/ency/patientinstructions/000355.htm

Ruston, D. (2016). *Screenagers* [Film]. MyDOC Productions.

References

Chapter 4

Should Teachers Be Replaced With Technology?

by
Maria Genova

[Yasmin and Daisha are in the music room at school, discussing their upcoming orchestra concert.]

Yasmin: I'm so nervous! Ms. Merkin keeps harping on me about that diminished B-flat. I never get what I'm doing wrong. Lately, I feel like I don't even want to play anymore.

Daisha: You mean quit orchestra? I thought you loved violin more than anything. What's going on?

Yasmin: I don't know. I feel like Ms. Merkin's so rushed to meet the standards. She doesn't really take time to show anybody their parts.

Daisha: You're supposed to practice on your own.

Yasmin: I know—I do. But it seems like whenever I practice, I mess up, and I can't figure out how to do it right.

Daisha: Hmm . . . have you tried Music Wizard? It's this really cool app that shows you scales and how to position your fingers correctly. It will even listen to you play and tell you if you're in key. I use it all of the time!

Yasmin: I don't know. Those learning apps are so mechanical. I miss the orchestra teacher at my old school, Mr. Zahn. He would always tell us about the music—why he chose it, why it was important, what it meant to him.

DOI: 10.4324/9781003238393-6

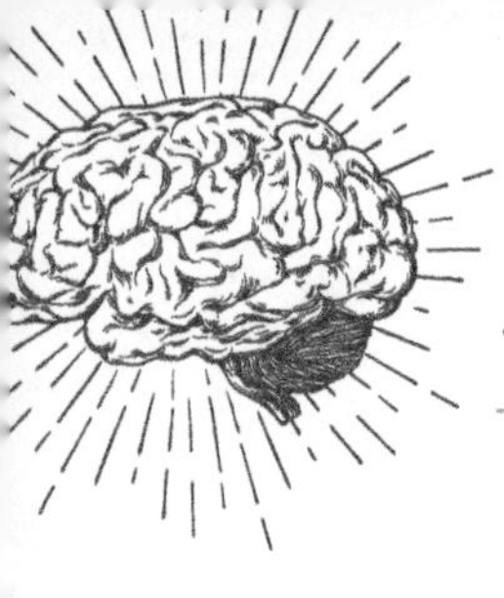

And he took us to play for these people at a retirement home. They loved it so much. One lady cried and hugged him at the end. I always seemed to get it right for Mr. Zahn—or at least he didn't harp on me if I didn't. It seemed fun. Now it just seems like work.

Daisha: That kind of teacher is hard to find. Ms. Merkin has way too many students to mess around.

Yasmin: Why is enjoying the music "messing around"?

Daisha: Music is very mathematical. On Music Wizard you earn points for every correct rendition, and you can redeem your points for music downloads. So, I practice over and over. The repetition will help you get it right.

Yasmin: But, Daisha, don't you think there's more to learning than getting it right?

Daisha: Like what?

Yasmin: Like inspiration.

Daisha: Getting it right is all the inspiration I need.

Technology has been crucial to humans' success as a species. Some technologies have been as simple as the wheel, and others as advanced as the airplane. Technology continues to push the limits of the imagination. Dedicated research into the field of artificial intelligence has already produced digital assistants, like Siri and Alexa, that can do so many things for people—more and more each day.

One job that certainly needs digital assistance is teaching. Teachers in the United States are notoriously overworked and underpaid. Their job is extremely important yet extremely difficult. They have to keep 25 individuals safe and happy while enabling them to pass the next test. No wonder, then, that teachers increasingly rely on videos, SMART Boards, computer tutorials, behavior management software, digital testing, and a host of other technologies designed to make the learning process easier for everyone.

As use of technology in the classroom increases, the role of the teacher decreases. Is this a good thing? In the dialogue, Yasmin speaks of a teacher who inspired her to learn. Every person has had a teacher like that at some point in their lives. Will technology edge these special people out? What then? Will technology be able to inspire students like those teachers did? Daisha seems to think it can. Should teachers be replaced with technology?

Your answer to this question will depend on how you think humans learn. If the human brain is essentially a machine, then it can be programmed like a machine, and a machine is the most logical tool to do the programming. But if there is a more spiritual element to the human mind that responds to feelings and creativity, then machines will never be up to the task. Philosophers are split on this issue. This chapter looks at each side in turn.

Psychological behaviorism is a theory that casts the human mind as a machine. According to this view, humans learn by responding to stimuli in their environment. Their success provides positive reinforcement, and their mistakes provide negative reinforcement. Consider, for instance, a toddler with a shape sorter. She may first try to put a square peg into a round hole. When this action is unsuccessful, she reinforces the idea that square shapes are different from round holes. When she successfully inserts the square peg in the square hole, she reinforces the idea that square shapes fit into square holes, thereby achieving a better understanding of the properties of squares.

Operant conditioning: Teaching by giving rewards for good behavior and punishment for bad behavior.

American psychologist B. F. Skinner used behaviorism to build a new conception of education. Skinner saw all learning as behavior that can be controlled through a system of rewards and punishments. If a behavior produces a positive outcome, students will be motivated to repeat the behavior. If a behavior produces a negative outcome, students will be motivated not to repeat it. Therefore, the job of the teacher is to be sure that the right rewards and punishments are in place. Through this operant conditioning, educational experiences "program" students to exhibit the desired learning behaviors.

Skinner noted, however, that it is difficult to set up an effective system of rewards and punishments in the traditional classroom. When a teacher introduces a math concept, for example, they must convey their lesson to 25 students at different skill levels. Some students master the concept immediately and need to be rewarded right away to reinforce their success. Meanwhile, others need more time and instruction. Some may even need punishment in order to discourage distracting behavior. Rewards and punishment must be delivered immediately in order for the students to make the correct association between their behavior and its outcome. As one person teaching 25 students, how will the teacher deliver the correct mix of rewards and punishments in a timely fashion?

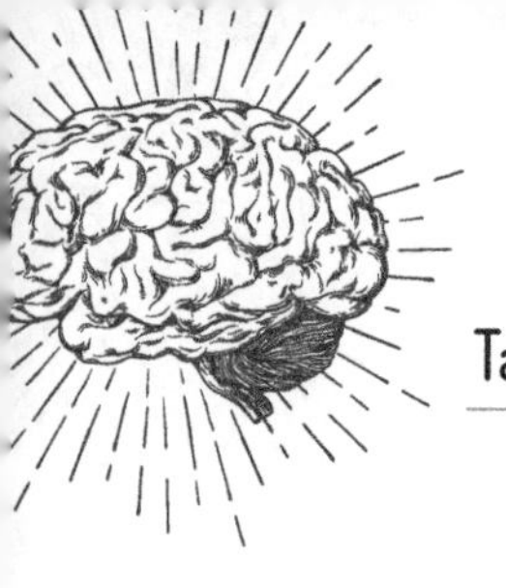

Skinner developed vision for a teacherless classroom. He insisted that students need to be able to learn material in small steps, mastering each step and being rewarded for it, before moving on to the next one. Because it would be difficult or even impossible for a teacher to deliver this kind of learning experience to a room full of students, Skinner developed a teaching machine that could do so. This was more than 60 years ago, before the invention of the Internet. Since then, Skinner's basic concept of a teaching machine has taken off. Online teaching tools are able to teach new skills, test them, and provide reinforcement—which can be as simple as a green checkmark for correct answers and a red x for incorrect answers. This saves human labor and allows students to proceed at their own pace. Advancements in technology, such as artificial intelligence, will continue to improve these programs.

Proponents of technology in the classroom also claim to be able to provide better source material. Without technology, teachers have to determine their own way of conveying the information in the textbook, but they may be unlikely to have the time or expertise to do a good job. Why not rely on experts to develop lesson plans in technology modules that can be used in classrooms across the country? For instance, Harvard professors could develop a curriculum with interactive videos and exercises for use in public schools. This would allow students who can't afford an expensive school to learn from a high-quality program. It would also promote greater consistency across the U.S. education system.

Skinner's Argument *FOR* Technology

1. Students learn most effectively when their teachers individualize positive and negative reinforcement for them.
2. Humans cannot individualize positive and negative reinforcement for students.
3. Technology can individualize positive and negative reinforcement for students.
4. Therefore, technology is a more effective teacher than humans.

Although some argue that technology can perform many functions of teachers, if not replace them entirely, others insist on retaining the human element. American philosopher John Dewey believed that the educational process is not only psychological, but also social and experiential.

Dewey demonstrated the social aspect of education through a young child learning to speak. The child begins by babbling. Through interacting with others, the child connects the babblings to social experiences. For example, the child says, "mama," and the mother smiles warmly, saying, "Yes, I'm your mama." Notice that the child is not just associating a word with an object—something any computer could teach. The child is learning about love and relationships—something no computer could teach. The same is true of every word the child learns. When the word *spider* is introduced, is it introduced with fear or with awe? When the word *sex* is introduced, is it introduced with embarrassment or with respect? Social values come hand-in-hand with everything kids learn. It is the teacher's job

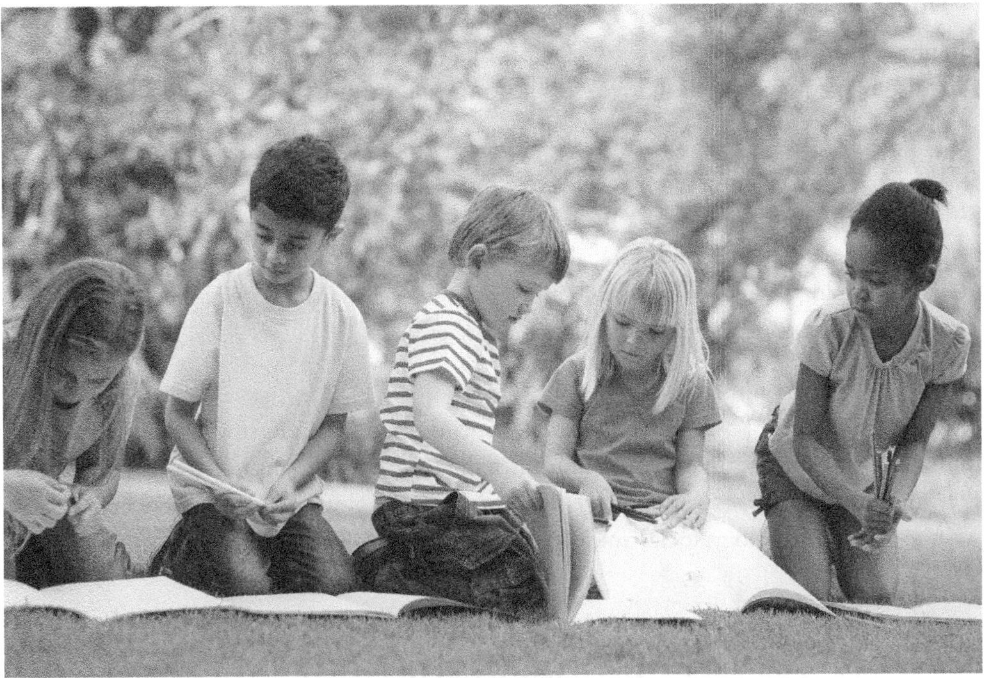

to convey healthy values along with information. Technology, by contrast, strips interpersonal value from the information, rendering it socially meaningless.

Dewey's concern about the experiential aspect of learning can be demonstrated through growing a bean plant. Imagine a student planting a seed, watering it each day, watching it grow, measuring its dimensions, picking its beans, eating them, comparing them to beans grown in different soil, and so on. Now imagine a student learning about plants through a computer simulation. First of all, the simulation is likely to take 10 minutes as opposed to 10 days. Technology is always speeding things up and eliminating wait time. Is this a good thing? Or is it good to learn patience and delayed gratification, which are so often needed in natural settings?

Second, the technology eliminates unforeseen disasters, such as a neighboring dog digging up the seed. Yes, the computer simulation could be programmed with a number of "surprises." But it cannot replicate a true surprise because computers are inherently predictable. The teacher, at any rate, will not be surprised and will thereby lose the opportunity to demonstrate problem solving. This goes against Dewey's vision, because he believed that it is not until people are faced with a real problem that they wake up and think.

Third, will the computer simulation enable the student to smell the blossoms, hear the water soaking the soil, feel the delicate leaves, and taste the delicious beans? Probably not. Yes, computer simulations are getting more and more realistic. Perhaps in 50 years there will be virtual gardens that are indistinguishable from the real thing. But for now losing the sensory stimulation that naturally accompanies information is tragic. It makes learning dry, boring, and meaningless.

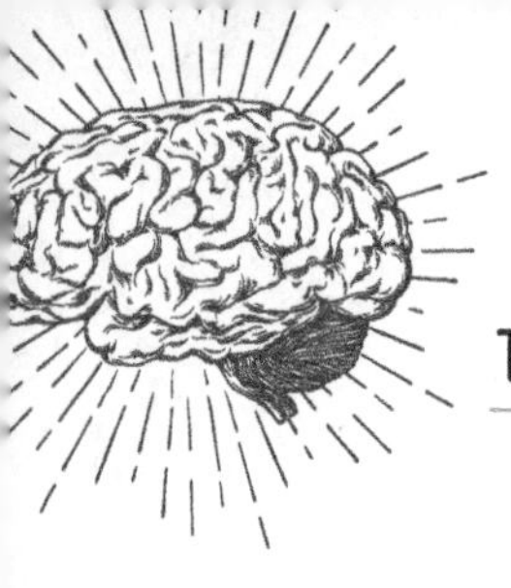

The process of learning that Dewey envisioned requires a human teacher and a natural, physical environment. These two factors make learning inefficient and frustrating, but they also make students fall in love with learning and inspire them to be lifelong learners.

Dewey's Argument *AGAINST* Technology

1. The best teacher provides social and experiential learning.
2. Technology is incapable of providing genuine social and experiential learning.
3. Therefore, technology is not the best teacher.

The arguments of Skinner and Dewey depend upon different understandings of how humans learn. As researchers gain more insight into human psychology and the brain, they may find new ways to approach education. As technology develops, there may be new ways to make technology social and experiential.

Personal Statement

In my experience, both Skinner and Dewey are right in some ways. Certain technologies have been indispensable to my learning. For instance, Google Docs has allowed me to collaborate with people I have never even met. I am also interested in the idea of using video games in education. A video game can immerse students in a story in an interactive way. It could allow students to learn in a low-risk environment while making subject matter interesting and relevant to their lives. However, at the same time, I also value old-fashioned group work, sitting around a table and getting to know people. Although I see technology as having much potential for teaching, I wouldn't want it to completely replace teachers or social learning situations.

Discussion Questions

1. How would your learning experience be different without contact with your teachers?
2. Do you feel there are certain technologies that are indispensable to your education?
3. Would reliance on technology hinder the development of certain skills, such as cursive writing or longhand arithmetic? Make a list of disadvantages.
4. Would reliance on technology eliminate certain problems, such as the spread of contagious illness or pollution from school busses and minivan drop-off? Make a list of advantages.
5. Can you think of a good middle ground between Skinner's and Dewey's views? Would a hybrid classroom be the best solution?

Classroom Activities

1. Learn your next math unit using an app or educational software (you may be able to find a free one through your library). At the end, discuss the pros and cons of this unit compared to traditional teaching.
2. Write a letter to a teacher who has inspired you. Let them know what they did that made learning meaningful for you.

References

Dewey, J. (1973). The child and the curriculum. In J. J. McDermott (Ed.), *The philosophy of John Dewey* (pp. 497–482). The University of Chicago Press.

Graham, G. (2019). Behaviorism. In E. N. Zalta (Ed.), *The Stanford encyclopedia of philosophy* (Spring 2020 ed.). https://plato.stanford.edu/entries/behaviorism

Skinner, B. F. (1961). Why we need teaching machines. *Harvard Educational Review, 31,* 377–398.

PART II
MENTAL HEALTH

Chapter 5

What Is the Meaning of Life?

by
Oliver Golias

There once was a young man plagued by the questions of life. He would wonder, "Is the world around me real? Do my senses deceive me? What about magic and powers unseen? Why must people toil and suffer? Is there any meaning or purpose to my existence?" Of all of these questions, the last bothered him the most. He set off to find an answer.

First he consulted his town's elders. They retorted, "Why, your purpose is to support the community! You must strive to enhance this society." So, he began to volunteer all around town, building shelters for those less fortunate and working for the betterment of those around him. But his heart still questioned.

One day, when he felt low, he came across a priest. He asked the priest about his purpose. He was told: "Serve the church. Those who love God shall inherit the peace of His Kingdom." So, the young man began a religious life—praying, worshipping God, and serving the church in any way he could.

Although each of these answers granted its own form of fulfillment, his questioning continued. Journeying to another city, he found an atheist who seemed surprisingly peppy. The troubled young man could not help but ask, "Why am I here? Certainly you, who remain cheerful without a godly purpose, must have some insight." The atheist responded, "There is no reason for

 DOI: 10.4324/9781003238393-8

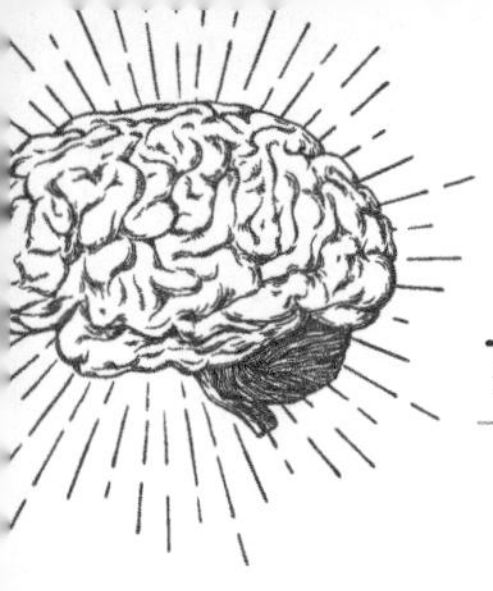

> our existence. You and I are only accidents before a faceless void. But we can still create fulfillment through art and literature and science!"
>
> At this, the young man's mind was addled like never before. He sought fulfillment in all things recommended to him, sometimes appearing to find it. But even then, he could not stop questioning.
>
> Finally, he sought out a great sage amongst the spirits of the woods. After a grueling journey, he posed his question once more. The sage, in a most unfazed manner, responded, "You need a purpose? Bah! Let me ask you: What makes you think you'll find a purpose in this world?"

Does this parable feel familiar to you? Do you find yourself wondering about the meaning of life? At the end of the parable, the sage raises some further questions: Do people have a purpose? Do people need a purpose? How will they ever know, one way or another?

Philosophers have explored these questions for thousands of years. Two of the most famous are devout Christian Søren Kierkegaard and atheist Albert Camus. Kierkegaard believed that, although people cannot know their purpose, they achieve a meaningful life by serving God. Camus, on the other hand, contended that people have no purpose and must create meaning based on the few things they can be certain of. Whether you are a theist, an atheist, or anything in between, these philosophers provide insight as to how you can find an answer for yourself.

Kierkegaard believed that people cannot find any meaning in life until they hit bottom with complete and total despair. In fact, Kierkegaard actually recommended despairing of life as a good thing to do! Only in despair, he thought, when people finally reject all of their daily distractions, do they discover true faith in God. Kierkegaard recognized three steps to despair: (1) not knowing one's purpose, (2) willing a purpose, and then (3) abandoning that purpose. The young man in the parable undergoes these three steps repeatedly. Kierkegaard would tell the young man that his mistake was in failing to hit bottom so that he could discover true faith in God.

Kierkegaard demonstrated what it means to hit bottom and find true faith through the biblical story of Abraham and Isaac. In this story, God told Abraham to sacrifice his son Isaac atop a sacred mountain. By "sacrifice" God meant "kill." This was an astonishing order. Abraham could not tell his son what they were

Søren Kierkegaard

doing as they travelled for 3 days to the mountain without bringing a goat to sacrifice. After preparing an altar, Abraham tied up his son and prepared to slit his throat. At the last minute, an angel descended to tell Abraham that because his faith was true, God had decided to provide a goat for the sacrifice instead.

Abraham's long journey to the altar is one of the most anxiety-inducing situations imaginable. He faced an impossible choice: either disobey God or kill his son. He was completely uncertain of what he should do. He had to blindly trust God, setting aside his own rational thoughts.

Kierkegaard felt that Abraham set a great example because true faith is an irrational passion. There is no rhyme or reason to it; one just has to leap into the darkness. The moral Kierkegaard wished to draw from the Abraham story is that all people need to make that leap in order to make their lives meaningful. Just as Abraham's faith enabled him to endure the journey to the altar, faith will enable anyone to endure the uncertain journey of life. Just as God rewarded Abraham with a goat for the sacrifice, God will reward the faithful with an afterlife in heaven.

Kierkegaard's Argument

1. True faith in God enables people to overcome despair.
2. Overcoming despair is what makes life meaningful.
3. Therefore, true faith in God makes life meaningful.

Camus's complaint against this argument was that Kierkegaard took life too seriously, casting his life as a drama straight out of the Old Testament. Why not cast it as an episode of *SpongeBob SquarePants* instead? This may seem absurd, but Camus insisted that a SpongeBob story is no more absurd than the Abraham story. Who is to say which is ultimately more meaningful? How can anything in life be ultimately meaningful, given that everyone will die someday anyway?

Because Camus doubted the existence of God and an afterlife, he had to find meaning within a world of seemingly meaningless activity. Camus described human lives as a grind with no inherent value. For example, by going to school, students keep progressing, but every bit of progress requires more progress. Each new math unit leads to a test, which leads to a new unit, which

Albert Camus

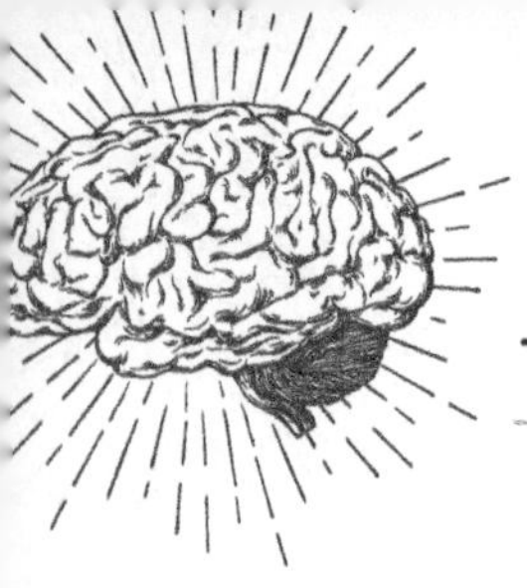

leads to a test. Even after students finally graduate, their career will present them with a similar cycle of anxiety.

Although Kierkegaard was content to wait for death to be finally released from the cycle of anxiety, Camus looked for moments of release *within* the cycle of anxiety. He illustrated this perspective through the myth of Sisyphus. In Greek mythology, Sisyphus was the king of Corinth. Because Sisyphus had cheated death, the gods wanted to punish him. So they condemned him to push a boulder up a hill all day until he reached the top. At the end of the day, the gods would push the boulder back down the hill so that Sisyphus would have to start all over the next day. According to the gods, Sisyphus's true punishment lay in those moments when he was aware of the uselessness of this task. It seems the gods succeeded in inventing the ultimate torment.

But Camus gave two reasons why Sisyphus might still remain content or even cheerful during this process. The first is that each day Sisyphus really does accomplish a goal—the goal of successfully pushing a boulder up a hill. This feat alone gives him something to boast of and strive toward. Similarly, students are condemned to study for the sake of continual studying, but they achieve greater knowledge through that work. Learning anything is something to be proud of, and continual learning is an admirable goal.

The second reason Sisyphus might remain cheerful is that he gets to walk down the hill at the end of each day. On the way down, he can take in the view. He can feel the grass upon his feet. He can find flowers and feel the wind pass through his hair. Similarly, students have time after school and on the weekends to enjoy life.

This second reason is striking. According to the gods, Sisyphus's respites are his real punishment, because that is when he is most painfully aware that he has to push the boulder up the hill again. The walk down the hill is intended to make him curse his fate of repeating the task. Likewise, when people are hard at work, they hardly ever notice that their work is futile; it is when they are at rest that they suddenly see the absurdity of their situation and hate knowing that it must continue. But hatred is a choice. People don't have to hate the knowledge of their situation. Camus portrayed Sisyphus as choosing to be happy instead. By embracing the cycle he is condemned to repeat, he can begin to enjoy himself. He has the ability to turn from anxiety to pleasure.

Camus's philosophy starts with the premise that people will never know their true purpose. In fact, given the absurdities they face, it is likely that they have no purpose. Even so, they have the ability to create meaning by achieving goals and enjoying the unending continuation of striving.

Camus's Argument

1. People can choose to enjoy striving.
2. Choosing to enjoy striving creates meaning in people's lives.
3. Therefore, people can create meaning in their lives.

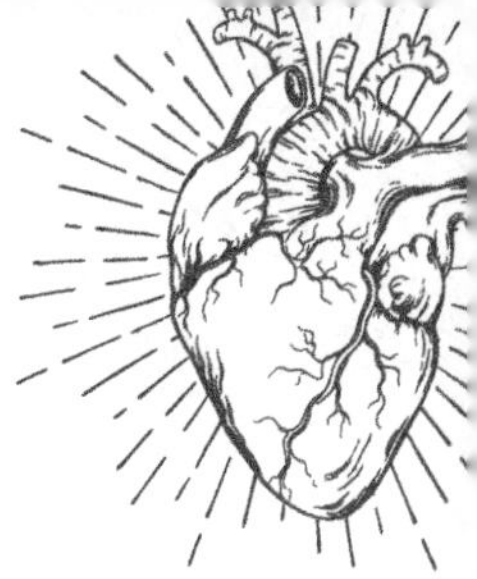

Personal Statement

Of these two arguments, I find Camus's to be stronger, although they are close contenders. They are both based on the realization that all people are uncertain of their purpose. Camus claimed intermittent respites are the source of personal meaning, while Kierkegaard asserted that personal meaning comes from looking forward to the afterlife. Although these are both perfectly valid, I would rather invest in brief moments that I know exist than hold out hope for an afterlife that seems doubtful to me.

Kierkegaard's model citizen is Abraham, who quelled his anxiety through faith that God's plan would be superior to his own. Assuming this story is true, this testament to faith is astounding and rightfully praised. But the ability to hold such a faith is seldom found in humanity. Kierkegaard acknowledged that the faithless call those who are faithful "fools" because they are willing to believe in what seems unrealistic. If one assumes that God exists, such faith must be the true path to happiness, but if there is no God, the faithful must be fools.

Both of these theories teach people how to grope their way out of anxiety without the need to know their purpose. As the sage tells the young man in the parable, "What makes you think you'll find a purpose in this world?" All people wonder what they should be doing with their lives. Few receive a definite answer. Whether you are a theist or an atheist, there are ways to answer this question for yourself without needing to know for sure.

Discussion Questions

1. What do you think of Kierkegaard's suggestion that despair is a good thing? Do you think it is necessary to hit bottom before finding the meaning of life? Why or why not?
2. What do you think about Camus's assertion that human life is absurd? Does your life feel pointlessly repetitive? Explain.
3. Is it reasonable to assume people cannot find the meaning of life through rationality? If they can, why do you think philosophers cannot agree on a universal purpose?
4. Suppose Kierkegaard is right, and the only escape from anxiety is "irrational passion." How do you think you could access this passion? Can you think of any ways this passion could be achieved outside of a religious context?
5. Suppose Camus is right, and choosing to enjoy life's absurdities creates meaning. What does this look like to you? Is it possible for Camus's theory to fit within a religious perspective?

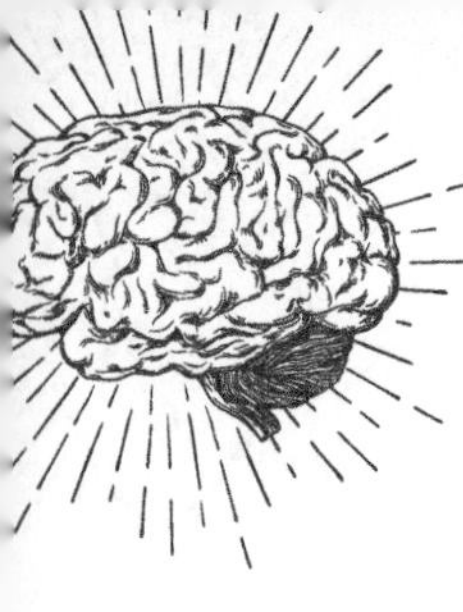

Classroom Activities

1. Write and share stories that express the purpose in your life. You can cast your life as an episode of a silly TV show, like SpongeBob SquarePants, or as a serious epic, like the Bible.
2. Make a painting or drawing of Sisyphus. Convey whether or not he finds his life meaningful and why.

References

Camus, A. (2018). *The Myth of Sisyphus and other essays* (J. O'Brien, Trans.). Vintage International. (Original work published 1955)

Kierkegaard, S., & Lowrie, W. (2013). *Fear and trembling and the sickness unto death* (Rev. ed., W. Lowrie, Trans.). Princeton University Press. (Original work published 1941)

Chapter 6

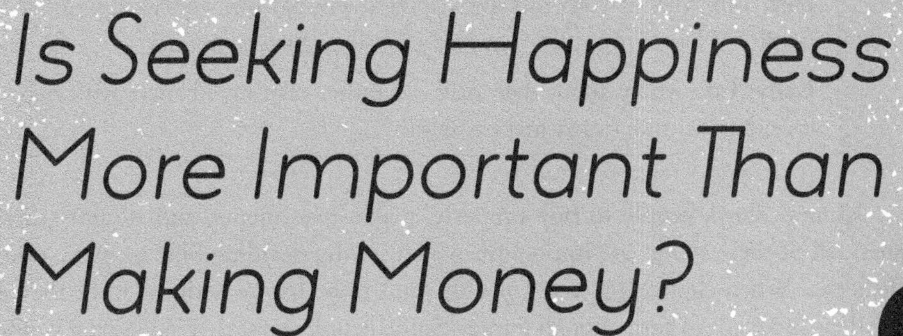

Is Seeking Happiness More Important Than Making Money?

by
Rachel C. Lee

[Kelly and Dee are driving home from school.]

Kelly: I'm so excited for college next year. I still can't believe I got accepted! How about you?

Dee: I'm not really excited. It's going to be so much hard work.

Kelly: What do you mean? Can't you take classes that you'll like?

Dee: Not really. I plan on majoring in chemistry. It'll probably suck, but at least when I'm out of there I'll make plenty of money.

Kelly: Geez, if you don't like chemistry, maybe you shouldn't major in it. I haven't even decided yet. But I plan on majoring in something I love, like history.

Dee: Well, I want to be happy *after* I graduate college. For me, that'd mean having enough money for an apartment downtown and a cool electric car. A chemistry major will get me a job that pays well. I don't know about history, though . . .

Kelly: Having plenty of money would be nice, but I don't think money would make up for doing something I hate every day. Once you get your chemistry degree, you'll have to work a job that includes the same stuff you hated in college.

 DOI: 10.4324/9781003238393-9

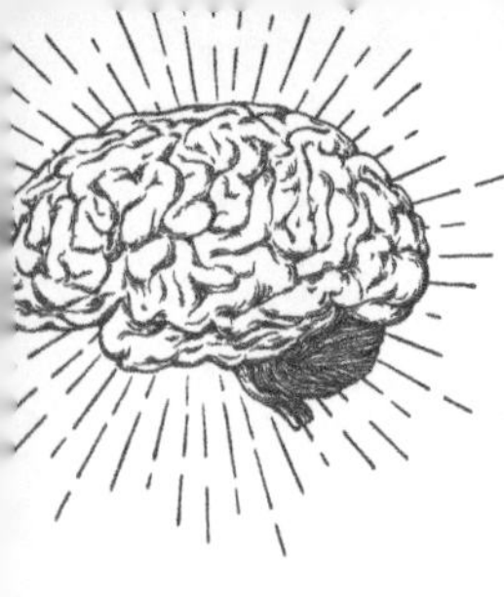

> **Dee:** Yeah, that might be a problem, but a job is a job. It'll always be difficult in some way.
>
> **Kelly:** Even if my job is difficult, as long as it involves history, I'll love it! History is my passion. I want history in my life.
>
> **Dee:** But what if your job doesn't make enough for you to support a family? What if you can't even *find* a job for a history major?
>
> **Kelly:** I do worry about that. Still, I'd rather take my chances with history than assume I can't make it work.

Money allows people to buy property, make investments, and support their loved ones. All of these things are important, which is why deciding how to make money is a challenge. When choosing a career, people want to be happy with the work they will do, but they also want to earn enough money. Some people insist that "following your dream" is more important than living comfortably, while others stress that a good job is one that pays well. Have you ever had a relative or friend tell you that doing what you love is better than making a lot of money? What about the opposite? There are strong, educated opinions on both sides of the issue.

Before considering whether doing what you love or making money is more important, think about whether a person can have both. Some of the wealthiest movie stars, pop stars, and athletes in the United States were able to find a path in life that indulged their passion and also made them plenty of money. For example, LeBron James loved basketball, worked hard at it, and made millions.

On the other hand, are these lucky few the happiest people in the world? Why do so many of them end up miserable? Consider Demi Lovato, who made it big on the Disney Channel and beyond while suffering from depression, an eating disorder, self-harm, and drug abuse. Would it have been better for her to have contented herself with enjoying music at a personal level?

More generally, does money corrupt? Nineteenth-century philosopher Henry David Thoreau said it does. Thoreau set out to discover how to live a fulfilling life. Realizing that society drags people into activities that make them miserable, he built a cabin for himself in the woods. Isolated in his cabin, he was able to focus on living as simply as possible. He wrote poetry and explored nature instead of working a normal job. Thoreau also wrote a book called *Walden* that urges people to do what they love and use as little money as possible.

Henry David Thoreau

Although people often argue that having both money and an enjoyable lifestyle is best, Thoreau said that money gets in the way of living life to the fullest. According to him, being caught up in the daily struggles of work and consumerism causes people to miss out on the real value of life, which is found in the appreciation of nature. Thoreau wrote:

> The mass of men lead lives of quiet desperation. What is called resignation is confirmed desperation. From the desperate city you go into the desperate country and have to console yourself with the bravery of minks and muskrats. A stereotyped but unconscious despair is concealed even under what are called the games and amusements of mankind. There is no play in them, for this comes after work. But it is a characteristic of wisdom not to do desperate things. . . . If you advance confidently in the direction of your dreams, and endeavor to live the life you have imagined, you will meet with the success unexpected in common hours.

Materialism: A tendency to consider material possessions and physical comfort as more important than spiritual values.

Consumerism: A social mindset in which people are encouraged to buy goods and services in ever-increasing amounts.

Thoreau warned against choosing a conventional lifestyle in which people commit to a profession that will make money. This lifestyle will leave them unfulfilled, in "unconscious despair." By being confident in living a different life (likely making less money), that despair can be avoided; the confident person will find success in their own way.

Do you think that by following Thoreau's advice, you would have a happier life? Consumerism and materialism are so common in society that most people hardly notice them. Yet, on closer examination, are they fulfilling? Thoreau found an alternative lifestyle that fulfilled him spiritually and emotionally.

Have you ever thought about how many things you own but don't need or use regularly? If the money you make just goes toward buying more of these things, is it worthwhile to make as much money as possible? Thoreau would say that it's not worthwhile. In his view, it would be much better to spend time finding intangible fulfillment—enjoyment of life through things that can't be bought.

Thoreau's Argument *AGAINST* Making Money

1. Doing what you love is more important than having lots of useless things.
2. Making money results in having lots of useless things.
3. Therefore, doing what you love is more important than making money.

Other philosophers have disagreed with Thoreau. Tara Smith argued that money *can* buy happiness. She explained that money can enhance a person's life because of the range of important ways that it can be spent. For instance, if a person uses money to fund their education, they are buying experiences that could lead to more fulfillment in life, which could make them happier. Because money can enhance life in this way, Smith referred to it as a *value*. Smith went on to argue that even if someone chooses a job they don't enjoy, they can still be happy about the money they are making, precisely because that money is

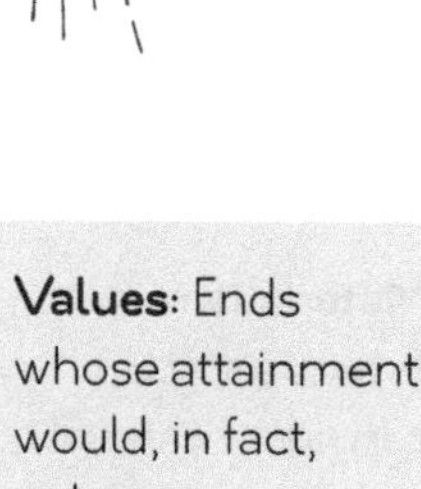

being spent on fulfilling things. Does this mean that finding a "dream job" isn't necessary for happiness?

Values: Ends whose attainment would, in fact, enhance a person's life.

Today's society requires people to spend money in order to survive. Most people would want to be independent and make enough money to support themselves, rather than live off the kindness of others. But having enough money to support oneself is not the same as being *wealthy*. Being wealthy is having more than a person (and their family) really needs.

Smith maintained that being wealthy is a worthy goal. Imagine that your job is not enjoyable, but you make enough extra money to buy beautiful works of art. Is it better to support and enjoy great art, or is it better to live like Thoreau did, without any material comforts, simply because working for those comforts might not be enjoyable? According to Smith, the enjoyment wealth brings makes an unenjoyable job worth it.

Smith's Argument *FOR* Making Money

1. Making a lot of money allows a person to buy fulfilling things during their free time.
2. Having fulfilling things in their free time is more important than doing what they love at work.
3. Therefore, making a lot of money is more important than doing what they love at work.

From Smith's viewpoint, choosing not to earn money results in missed opportunities. There are endless choices for how money can be spent, many of which could lead to happiness. Even if people choose not to spend money on things for themselves, they could still work toward bettering society as a whole. After all, each person benefits from society in so many ways—police protection, roads, schools, stores, parks—so shouldn't everyone try to give something back?

As it happens, Thoreau did give an extraordinarily valuable gift to society; his essay "Civil Disobedience" inspired Mahatma Gandhi and Martin Luther King, Jr., along with millions of other societal reformers around the world. But suppose Thoreau had not published that essay. If he had stuck to poetry (which he loved but was not very good at), he never would have made an impact.

Although Thoreau's life showcases the impact of an immaterial gift, Smith's opinion could still hold true. Imagine if Thoreau had found a way to make money through work, and then he supported his cause financially, which could have, in turn, brought him happiness. It's possible that his impact on society would have been greater. However, Thoreau's chosen lifestyle left him so poor that he had no opportunity to use money for the sake of happiness.

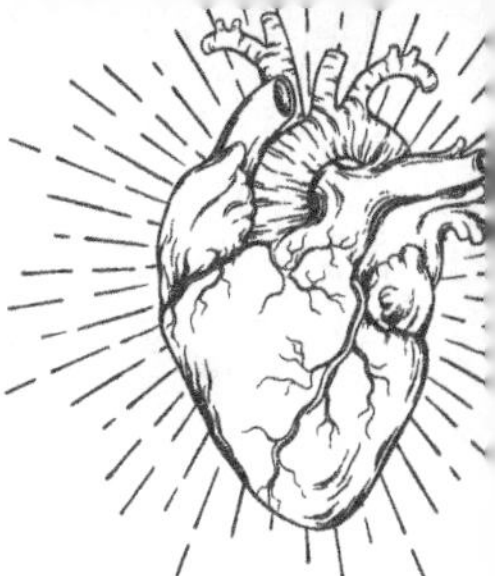

Thought Experiment

Imagine that you spend your college career studying both poetry and medicine. After you graduate you continue to love writing poetry, but find you don't enjoy being a doctor. Now you are starting a family and have to make a choice: continue working as a doctor to make money and contribute to society, or focus on poetry to enjoy your life. Is it better for you to be wealthy and unhappy or poor and happy? Which is better for your family?

Personal Statement

Just like art students and history majors, writers are known for doing what they love, not for making money. As an English major, I'm often told that my choice to pursue a subject I love might make it harder to earn money. Rather than focusing on a mainstream career path, I've chosen to focus my ambitions on becoming a games writer—composing the storylines and dialogues in video games. Majoring in English has been one of the first steps in that process.

College is expensive, and job opportunities for English majors are not guaranteed. However, I figure that if many people are discouraged from pursuing their dream major, and focus on making money through business or science, then maybe I will have less competition in doing what I love.

Even if I don't land a job with a comfortable salary, I want to embrace the idea of living frugally—not spending much more than what I need. For me, saving money while doing work that I love is not miserable by any means. Other people obviously feel differently; they would be happier with enough money to spend freely, even if they hate the job that sustains them. Ultimately, everyone's preference in career choices could be valid in its own way.

Growing up, I witnessed my father's frustration at working in a field that he couldn't always relate to. He didn't give up on past difficult jobs because he wanted to provide a stable life for my whole family. His father was an artist and couldn't always put food on the table for his family, but he was able to do what he loved because of that sacrifice. Each life choice has its own benefits and challenges.

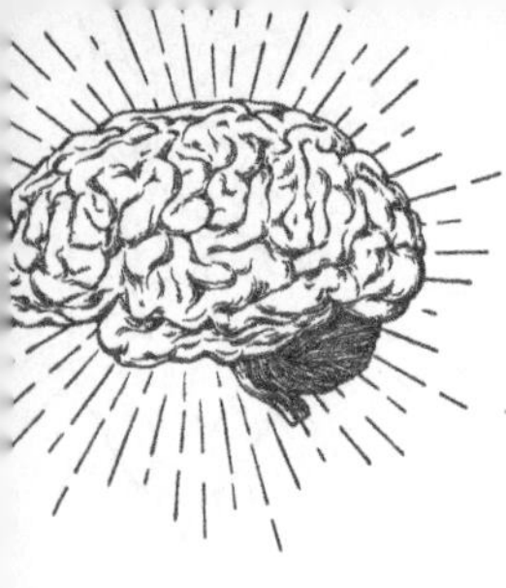

Discussion Questions

1. Think of a job that you would love to do and one that you would hate to do. Which job would make more money? Is it possible to do what you love and make substantial money at the same time?
2. Would you be willing to give up most of your possessions and live off the grid as Thoreau did? Would you value your possessions (and being able to afford new ones) more than experimenting with a lifestyle that allows you to do what you love?
3. If a younger friend or sibling asked you what job they should pursue, would you focus on how much money they would want to make or what they would enjoy doing? How might you be able to include both considerations in a conversation?
4. Think of a time when you were discouraged from pursuing a certain activity, such as going to an art school or playing in a band. Why do you think people tried to discourage you?

Classroom Activities

1. Hold a talent show in which everyone shares their passion. Discuss ways of making your passions into careers or other ways of keeping them in your life.
2. Watch and discuss Noeline Kirabo's TED Talk "2 Questions to Uncover Your Passion—and Turn It Into a Career" (https://www.ted.com/talks/noeline_kirabo_2_questions_to_uncover_your_passion_and_turn_it_into_a_career).

References

Smith, T. (2008). *Money can buy happiness.* Ockham's Razor.

Thoreau, H. D. (1854). *Walden.* Ticknor and Fields.

Chapter 7

Are Prescription Drugs a True Path to Wellness?

by
Oliver Golias

[Monique and Ted are in the bleachers at a home football game. Their team scores, the buzzer sounds, and the crowd goes wild. Their team wins the game. As people start filing out, Monique pulls Ted aside.]

Monique: Hey, Ted, can I be real with you for a moment? I'm kind of going through something and need to talk with someone.

Ted: Yeah, of course. What's up?

Monique: So, last week, I didn't miss your party because I was out of town. I was honestly just kind of freaking out.

Ted: Freaking out? What do you mean? Like, nervous or something?

Monique: Like, full-blown panic attack.

Ted: Wow . . . I'm sorry to hear that. You could have just told me. I would have understood.

Monique: Well, here's the embarrassing part. I actually couldn't have told you, because my mom was the one texting you. I was in the hospital, and I've been on medication since.

Ted: Oh my gosh! Are you okay?

DOI: 10.4324/9781003238393-10

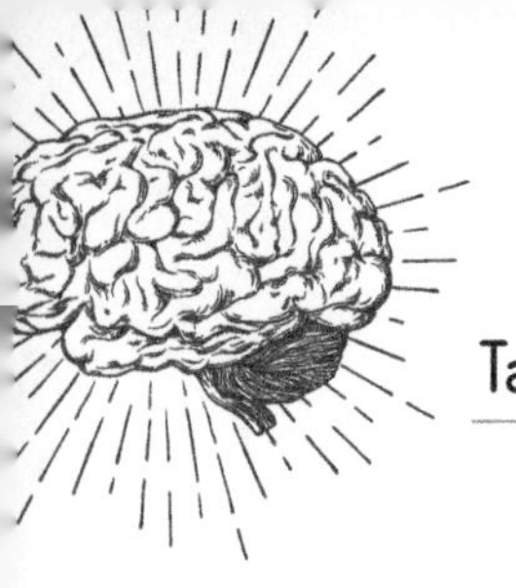

Monique: Yeah, I'm fine. It's just that the medication makes me feel sick all of the time.

Ted: That sucks. My dad says prescription drugs will screw up your brain. Maybe you should try something else. Have you tried meditation?

Monique: I feel like I've tried everything. The pills are the only thing that stop the panic. But I feel like they might be just covering something deeper, you know?

Ted: Maybe you're having a spiritual crisis. What about therapy? It would take a while, but you might get to the root of the problem.

Monique: Ugh—I don't know what to do . . .

Ted: Take some time to think about it. Whatever you decide is good as long as you're taking care of yourself.

In this dialogue, Monique and Ted have a type of conversation that seems to be more and more common among young people today. Monique is not well. Physically, she seems fine, but she's having emotional episodes that make it hard for her to function normally. Mental illness is a very serious issue that can be embarrassing to talk about. Fortunately, society is becoming more sympathetic toward mental illness and more proactive in treating it. But its causes still aren't fully understood. There are two major perspectives.

The first is that mental illness is caused by chemical imbalances within the brain. This perspective implies a view called *materialism*, or the theory that the universe is only made up of physically observable things. Mental faculties (thoughts and feelings) are really just the interaction of brain chemistry. According to the materialist view, balanced brain chemistry constitutes mental wellness.

The second perspective is that mental illness is caused by unhealthy beliefs and emotions. This implies a view called *dualism*, or the theory that the universe includes physical things as well as things made of some sort of spiritual or mental substance. Mental faculties exist on their own and are not directly affected by physical objects. According to the dualist view, healthy thoughts and feelings constitute mental wellness. This chapter will look at each of these perspectives in turn.

Materialism is prevalent within the sphere of medical professionals. The view implies that fixing the chemical imbalance will fix the illness itself. So, the solution, according to this view, is to prescribe drugs. Because drugs are substances that directly affect the chemical balance in the body, carefully crafted prescriptions could return the brain to its "normal" state.

There is no doubt that drugs have been successful in treating a wide variety of mental illnesses. Attention Deficit/Hyperactivity Disorder (ADHD) is the most commonly diagnosed mental health disorder among school-age children. In 2011, approximately 4.5 million children between ages 3 and 17 in the United States were reported as having ADHD. Of those, approximately 56% were taking medication to remedy their situation.

Nevertheless, some philosophers wonder whether any successfully treated individuals are ever truly healed.

ADHD causes a wide range of social and educational difficulties, including problems with attention span, impulse control, and hyperactivity. In reports of parents, teachers, and peers, medication improves students' behavior. But what does this improvement really mean? Are the students more cooperative, appropriate, or friendly? Does changing these outward behaviors count as changing people on the inside? Does it count as healing?

More severe mental disorders can involve issues far more serious than behavior. In the case of schizophrenia, for example, people often become completely unable to function in a social environment. Medication often restores their functioning and seems to improve their quality of life. Despite the demonstrated success of prescription drugs for schizophrenia, medical professionals typically insist that therapy must take place alongside medication to monitor results over time.

In a series of interviews, Rachel Miller and Susan Mason investigated the importance of medication for schizophrenic patients. They found that those who decided to discontinue their use of medication relapsed and were hospitalized. Miller and Mason concluded that schizophrenia can only be treated, not cured. This conclusion provides support for the materialist view that mental illnesses must be chemical. If medication can change one's brain chemistry to the point of mental stability, the problem must reside within the brain's chemical balance.

The Argument *FOR* Prescription Drugs

1. Medication balances brain chemistry.
2. Balanced brain chemistry constitutes mental wellness.
3. Therefore, medication is the true path to mental wellness.

On the other hand, mental processes do not seem mechanical in the way physical processes do. For example, if a person gets an infection, such as strep throat, they can take an antibiotic, such as penicillin. Antibiotics are physical substances that kill or disable germs—and this process can be viewed under a microscope. After the person completes the treatment, they will be physically healed. However, it is not possible to see how a panic attack works under a microscope. How does a physical substance kill a negative thought or neutralize a negative feeling? Mental processes seem to be intrinsically different from physical processes of the body. So, the dualist reasons that healing them must be different. Rather than using drugs, a dualist may turn to therapy or meditation to "recenter" how a

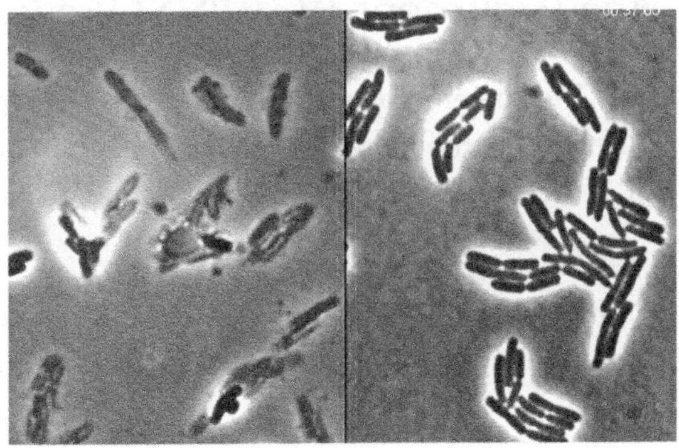

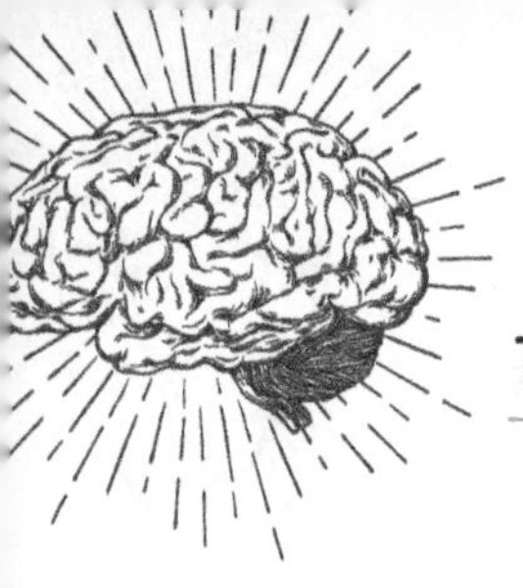

person thinks or feels. Eventually, these practices will turn into habits, and these habits will turn into a new state of mind.

A **placebo** is a fake pill used in scientific studies. In a **double-blind test**, neither the researcher nor the patients know who is receiving the real pill and who is receiving the fake pill. That way, their expectations won't skew the results of the study.

Stephen Flora pointed out an important problem with the research on prescription drugs: It often does not include a control group using placebos. Suppose that a researcher working with a group of patients with schizophrenia gives half of the patients the medication that is expected to work and the other half an identical-looking pill that does nothing. If the first group's symptoms improve, then such a study would verify that it is the medication, not merely the power of suggestion, that is helping the patients. However, such a study cannot easily be conducted. It would probably be unethical because half of the patients would not be receiving treatment.

Instead of medication, Flora recommended cognitive behavioral therapy, which is based on three main ideas:

* Mental illness is caused by faulty or unhelpful ways of thinking.
* Mental illness is caused by learned patterns of unhelpful behavior.
* People suffering from mental illness can learn better ways of thinking.

Although proponents of cognitive therapy are not necessarily dualists, their approach is consistent with the idea that human beings are more than just bodies. They have minds or spirits or souls that, when damaged, can only be healed in a nonphysical way.

In a study conducted in 2008, groups of adults diagnosed with ADHD attended a series of cognitive behavioral therapy sessions. These sessions covered what ADHD is, how it works, what emotional and relational maturity means, and problem solving. Carefully constructed surveys distributed before and after the study suggested great improvements in the patients' lives.

Cognitive behavioral therapy may also be helpful for more severe mental illnesses such as schizophrenia. One of the biggest problems for schizophrenic individuals undergoing prescription drug treatment is the side effects of their drugs. Cognitive therapy, in contrast, helps reduce negative episodes without compromising the patient's ability to enjoy life. Because cognitive behavioral therapy does not result in uncomfortable side effects, there is a much lower dropout rate amongst these patients, and 80% of those who completed treatment reported that they felt satisfied with the results. Observers reported significant reductions in symptoms.

The Argument *AGAINST* Prescription Drugs

1. Therapy promotes healthy thoughts and feelings.
2. Healthy thoughts and feelings constitute mental wellness.
3. Therefore, therapy is the true path to mental wellness.

A related path toward mental wellness is meditation. Although there are many types of meditation, one easy and accessible type is guided meditation. There are a variety of

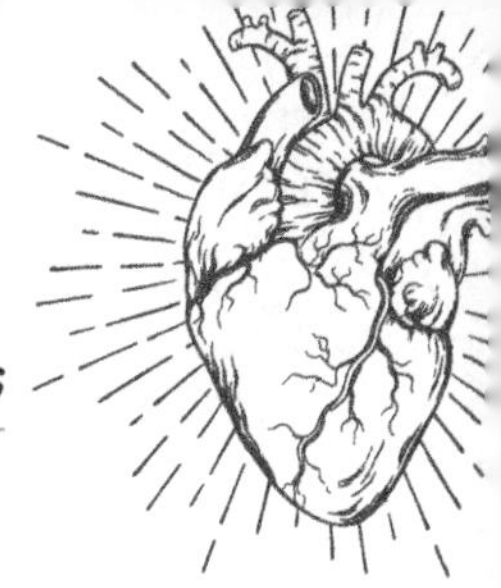

how-to videos on the Internet. Typically, a spiritual expert takes a person through the steps of relaxation and focus, encouraging them to strengthen their mind.

According to meditation enthusiasts, people can learn how to replace negative thoughts and feelings with peace and happiness. For those who find therapy too formal or too expensive, guided meditation may be the answer. Most meditation presupposes dualism; there is a strongly spiritual component to the human being that can be healed through spiritual exercises.

Personal Statement

I'm not sure whether the materialist or dualist view is correct. There is more scientific research to support the effectiveness of prescription drugs in reducing symptoms of mental illness. But I suspect this may be due to the fact that drugs provide a highly profitable market for doctors and psychiatrists.

Many people find that a combination of strategies works, but when beginning any prescription, be careful. Oftentimes, a new prescription may result in harm at first until the correct drug or dosage is found. Because of this, it is perfectly reasonable to want to avoid prescription drugs. However, if you are struggling with your mental health, you should still seek some form of help. This could be group/personal therapy, guided meditation, or both.

One thing is certain: Mental illnesses will not simply go away. The most important part of any path to wellness is to give it time to work. Especially for more severe mental disorders, therapy may not be enough to reduce symptoms to a high-functioning level. In these cases, prescription drug use is perfectly reasonable.

There is still a stigma surrounding drug use for mental health. Despite this, well-being should come first. Successful treatment is not the same as wellness, but it is better than nothing. Because effective prescriptions may take time to find, be sure to maintain contact with a doctor you trust. Eventually, a path to well-being can be found.

Discussion Questions

1. Do you consider yourself a materialist or a dualist? Why?
2. Do you think mental illness is an issue of brain chemistry or problematic thoughts and feelings? To what extent do these overlap?

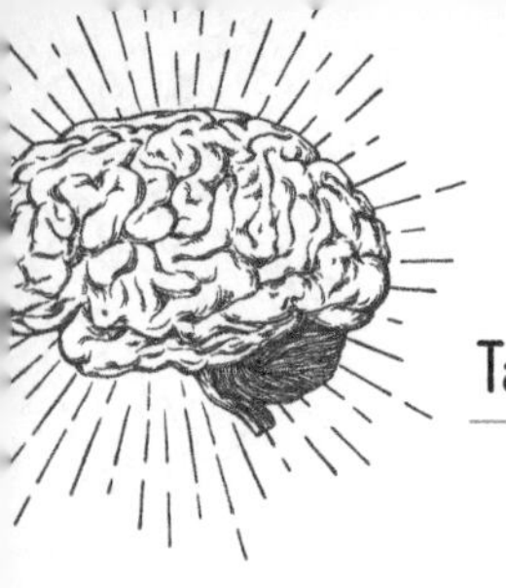

Discussion Questions, *continued*

3. Does the existence of a prescription drug industry make relying upon prescriptions problematic? How else could these drugs be distributed to safely benefit those who may need them?
4. Should parents be able to choose what type of treatment their adolescent children receive, or should the children decide? Are there exceptions to your conclusion?
5. Where do you think the stigma toward mental illness comes from? How can you respond to this stigma?

Classroom Activities

1. Practice meditation together with your class for a half hour each day for one week. At the end of the week discuss the pros and cons of the experience.
2. Research the mental illness that interests you most and make a presentation about it.

References

American Psychological Association. (2017). *What is cognitive behavioral therapy?* https://www.apa.org/ptsd-guideline/patients-and-families/cognitive-behavioral

Beck, A. T., & Rector, N. A (2000). Cognitive therapy of schizophrenia: A new theory for the new millennium. *American Journal of Psychotherapy, 54*(3), 291–300.

Bramham, J., Young, S., Bickerdike, A., Spain, D., McCartan, D., & Xenitidis, K. (2008). Evaluation of group cognitive behavioral therapy for adults with ADHD. *Journal of Attention Disorders, 12*(5), 434–441. https://doi.org/10.1177/1087054708314596

Flora, S. R. (2007). *Taking America off drugs: Why behavioral therapy is more effective for treating ADHD, OCD, depression, and other psychological problems.* State University of New York Press.

Miller, R., & Mason, S. (2011). *Diagnosis: Schizophrenia: A comprehensive resource for consumers, families, and helping professionals* (2nd ed.). Columbia University Press.

Ryan, J. B., Katsiyannis, A. & Hughes, E. M. (2011). Medication treatment for Attention Deficit Hyperactivity Disorder. *Theory into Practice 50*(1), 52–60. https://doi.org/10.1080/00405841.2010.534939

Chapter 8

Should Young People Be Allowed to Choose Their Own Religion?

by
Rachel C. Lee

[Kim runs into Carter at the movie theater.]

Kim: Hey, Carter! We missed you at church on Sunday. Where were you?

Carter: Oh, hi. Um—I've actually decided to take a break from church.

Kim: Uh-oh. What do your parents think?

Carter: Well, my mom is really upset about it, but my dad convinced her to let me try exploring other religions.

Kim: Well, be careful. Religion isn't a choice, like a restaurant or a movie or something. If you don't stay loyal to the religion you're given, you might end up lost and alone without any religion at all.

Carter: I'm going to look for God in other places. Maybe I'll like what I find, maybe not. I'm not worried. Plenty of people live happily without religion.

Kim: But if you're raised Christian, why would you turn away from such a gift? You should feel grateful that you're getting the truth from the beginning. I feel sorry for people in other countries who grow up with false religions and have to find the courage to leave them.

Carter: But don't you see how biased that is? They probably feel sorry for *you* in exactly the same way!

DOI: 10.4324/9781003238393-11

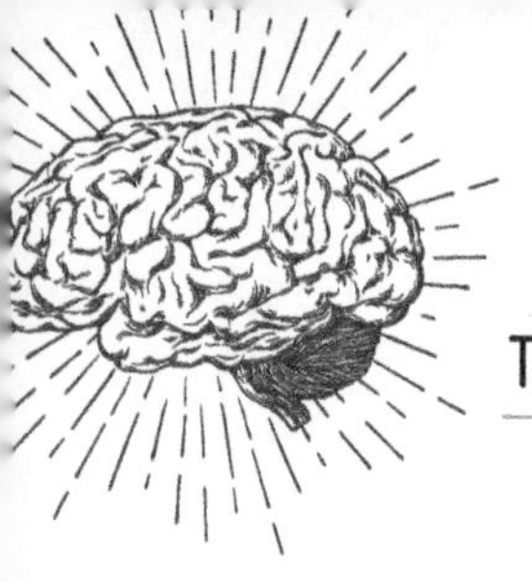

Kim: Maybe they do, but that just shows how wrong they are. Christianity is the only true religion.

Religion: A system of beliefs and practices grounded in the service of a god or supernatural power.

Carter: It works for you, and for a lot of people in this country, but not for everyone. What if another religion works better for me? I've always liked Shinto myths and legends. Maybe those values and beliefs will work better for me than the Christian ones do.

Kim: Carter, I go through times when geometry doesn't "work for me." That doesn't mean I get to dump geometry. It means I need to try harder to *make it work*! If you look deep in your heart, you'll know that the love of God your parents taught you is sacred.

Carter: Then you're really saying that our parents should determine our religion. What if my parents were delusional cultists who believe in human sacrifice? Should I have faith in *that* for the rest of my life?

Kim: If you pray to God, he will always help you find the truth.

Carter: *If* God exists. I guess I'm just going to have to find out.

Religion unifies people under a set of beliefs and creates communities in which people pray, celebrate, forgive, and support each other. Kids are usually raised to accept the same religion as their family. Some parents guide gently and allow for some disagreement; others expect rigid conformity. Still others don't promote any one religion at all; instead, they allow their kids to choose their own religion, if any. Have you ever known a young person to make their own decision about religion? Have you ever wanted to choose for yourself?

Religion reflects people's deepest values. This means that people who follow different religions might have completely different opinions on moral issues, such as how to be a good person or how to treat other people. Religion can also have a strong influence on the course of a person's life, such as who they marry (if anyone) and who they look up to (a rabbi, for example). Therefore, parents might want their child to grow up believing in the same religion as they do simply because the family will be more likely to get along and fit into the same social circle.

Parents typically love their kids and want to live in harmony with them. Religion is a way of creating and maintaining this harmony. Different religions can contradict each other. For example, Islam prohibits the drinking of alcohol, while Catholicism incorporates wine into its worship ritual. Because of this, some people believe there is a "right" religion and a "wrong" one. Allowing young people to choose their own religion could lead to painful conflict within or between families.

The question is whether the desire for shared values justifies indoctrination—forcing young people to accept religious beliefs without question. Mark Vopat argued that parents don't have the right to indoctrinate their kids with their religious beliefs. In his view, parents should have the privilege of sharing their belief without forcing it.

The difference between sharing one's belief and indoctrination is a fine line. Parents often bring their kids to their church, synagogue, or mosque every week. Does that count as forcing their religion? According to Vopat, the difference lies in whether parents try to shield their kids from alternative religions. He believed that it isn't in a young person's best interest to be exposed to only one religion. Preventing the child from appreciating a wide variety of options breeds resentment and narrowmindedness. Imagine that your parents were extremely strict about the music you listened to—so strict, in fact, that you could only listen to the piano, not guitar, vocals, or anything else. Maybe you would grow to love the piano. Or maybe you would start to resent the piano. Even if you felt no resentment toward the piano, do you think your life experiences would be lacking? Do you think your parents should have the right to restrict your childhood experiences this much? Vopat would say no.

Of course, every American citizen has the right to choose their own religion. This right is protected by the Constitution. But young people are not yet full-fledged citizens. They need a lot of civic education—learning about the U.S. government system, history, and political parties—before they are ready to vote at age 18. Likewise, don't they need a lot of religious education before they are ready to choose their own religion?

Perhaps so. This analogy would imply that kids should be educated in all religions of the world (Vopat would be in favor of this), but parents rarely do this. They are more likely to deliberately guide their kids into their own religion. This is like parents who require their child to take piano lessons every week. The child can listen to other instruments but must practice piano and perform it. The child is not allowed to quit. If it occurs to the child to ask for saxophone lessons instead, the parents will say no because they don't like saxophone music. They help their child with piano lessons, believing that the child will be grateful someday for acquiring this valuable expertise.

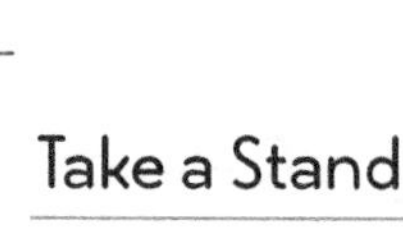

Vopat was concerned about two problems that arise with this kind of indoctrination:

1. Parents may prevent their kids from learning about other religions.
2. Parents may teach their kids that all other religions are false.

Faith: Accepting that something is true without conclusive proof.

He contended that both of these factors put young people at a disadvantage in a multicultural world. If young people are allowed to explore religion in their own way, they will be better prepared for positive encounters with different value systems.

Vopat's Argument *FOR* Religious Choice

1. Young people should be prepared to encounter different value systems.
2. Preparing to encounter different value systems means exploring other religions.
3. Exploring other religions may lead young people to choose their own religion.
4. Therefore, young people should be allowed to choose their own religion.

Philosopher Michael Hand shared Vopat's concern about indoctrination. In his view, however, indoctrination comes from misrepresenting the nature of religion. For Hand, parents have the right to firmly guide their kids into accepting their religion, as long as they explain that religion is a matter of faith rather than a matter of fact.

For example, the biblical story of Moses parting the Red Sea can't be proven true or false. Although there may be some evidence, and many people may believe in it, the Moses story is not taught in history books the way the story of Caesar crossing the Rubicon is. If parents teach the Moses story to their kids, they should teach it as a religious story, rather than as history. That way, there is no worry about indoctrination. When the kids grow up and begin to think independently from their parents, they can choose what to believe.

Hand argued that it is important for a child to experience what religious stories and rituals mean to people within that religion. This requires more than learning from a distance that Christians and Jews regard Moses as a prophet. It means developing a personal admiration for Moses and feeling his importance in one's life. Young people who are given nothing but an abstract introduction to all world religions will lack faith in any of them. They won't know what faith is and will not be spiritual people. On the other hand, young people who grow up sharing their parents' faith know what faith is and can transfer that faith to another religion when they grow up, if they wish.

Hand might worry that Vopat's idea of religious education is like a superficial musical education, in which a child is encouraged to try different instruments without ever being required to learn one instrument in depth. This child will never have a deep appreciation of music and will never know what it means to be a true musician. A child who is required to commit to piano, on the other hand, would eventually reach adulthood with the right to quit taking piano lessons and take up saxophone instead. With a lifetime of piano lessons, they could more fully appreciate the value of the piano and consider what they would be giving up if they chose to change. They may be likely to decide to continue on with piano because they have already invested so much in it. Even if they do change to saxophone, they will have relevant knowledge and experience to transfer. Either way, the parents feel good about providing a solid musical foundation.

Hand's Argument *AGAINST* Religious Choice

1. Choosing your own religion requires a full foundation in faith.
2. Young people don't achieve this full foundation until they reach adulthood.
3. Therefore, young people should not be allowed to choose their own religion.

Personal Statement

When I was about 7 years old, my dad would test his Photoshop skills by creating little booklets for me to read. One was filled with facts about Titan (one of Saturn's moons), and another was about how to pay better attention in school. One contained information on every major religion, complete with plenty of pictures. I was told that I could choose whichever religion I really connected with.

At the time, Shintoism appealed the most to me with its images of flying spirits and its value of nature. I told my dad that it was my favorite, but I never committed to it. I've come to appreciate many religions through studying their history and beliefs, but I've remained unaligned. I have been a speculator my whole life, imagining God and the supernatural but never believing through any religious lens. It almost seems too late to "choose" what I believe in, now that I have been thinking independently for so long.

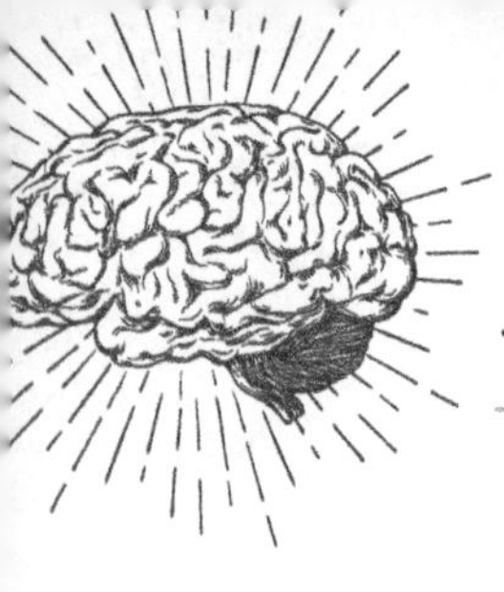

Still, I've never been completely comfortable as a nonreligious person. Sometimes I imagine an afterlife in which some higher power shouts, "Ha! You were supposed to have followed *that* religion all along!" Then I am banished to whichever hell that religion entails.

I also wonder if committing completely to one religion would somehow *make* that religion real for me, and my faith would be rewarded after death. Or I wonder if living without any religion is exactly what I am supposed to be doing with my life.

As much as life without religion can be a little confusing, I appreciate my parents' decision to let me experiment for myself and think freely about what I want to believe. I also admire the decision of other parents to introduce their kids to their religion in the hopes of guiding them and giving them happiness grounded in faith. But most of all, I admire young people who choose to think for themselves about what values matter most to them. Maybe they choose to seek these values in the religion they were raised with, or maybe they search for a religion with the values that feel right for them. Regardless, young people should never be afraid to think freely, especially about something so impactful as religion.

Discussion Questions

1. If you practice a religion, do you think it makes you closer to others in your religious community? Do you think that it divides you from people of other faiths? Is it possible that religion has had both of these impacts on you?
2. Imagine yourself as a parent. Would you want to give your kids any guidance on religion? Would you reflect any of your own parents' behavior, and why?
3. If a friend told you that they wanted to stop practicing their religion or change their religion, would you agree with their choice and/or support them? What if the religion they planned to stop practicing was your own?
4. Have your family's religious beliefs been at odds with your own? Conversely, have their beliefs ever given you guidance during an important time or event in your life?
5. Would you keep practicing a religion even if its teachings were consistently different from what you believed? Would you try to choose a religion based on the beliefs that you already have? Why or why not?

Classroom Activities

1. Interview a religious leader you admire concerning their view of faith versus freedom to choose. Share and discuss your interviews.
2. Create and share an online class magazine in which each person contributes a page about their religious beliefs. It could include an essay, poem, or story along with photos, drawings or other design elements.

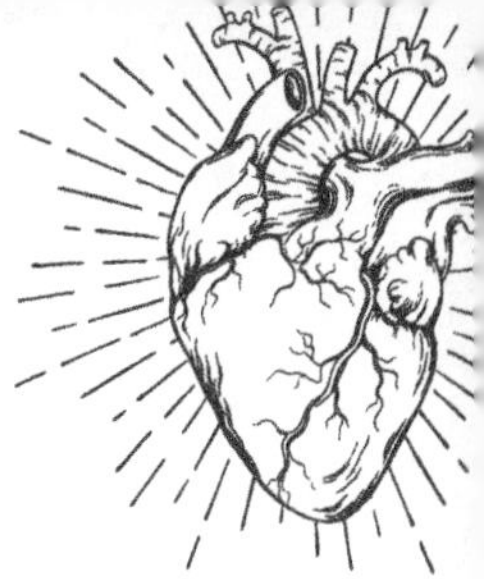

References

Hand, M., Mackenzie, J., Gardner, P., & Tan, C. (2004). Religious upbringing: A rejoinder and responses. *Journal of Philosophy of Education, 38*(4), 639–662. https://doi.org/10.1111/j.0309-8249.2004.00410.x

Vopat, M. (2009). Justice, religion, and the education of children. *Public Affairs Quarterly, 23*(3), 203–225.

PART III

RELATIONSHIPS

Chapter 9

What Is the Purpose of Friendship?

by
Dominic Fasano and
Eric Johnston

[Ken and Rita are at Dale's birthday party. It's a beach barbeque. A bunch of kids are sitting in groups around a bonfire, eating cake and talking. Ken goes to the buffet table for another piece of cake.]

Ken: Hey, Rita, I dare you to chuck this piece of cake at that geek over there.

Rita: Oh my God, Ken, what is your problem?

Ken: Come on, Rita, we've got to do something to save this party. Nobody wants to play volleyball, and the Jet Ski ran out of gas before I got a turn. The food wasn't even as good as it usually is at Dale's parties. What a waste of time.

Rita: Quit feeling sorry for yourself. You're not here for *you*. You're here for *Dale*.

Ken: What's that supposed to mean?

Rita: It's Dale's birthday, dummy. You're here to celebrate his life and show him you care about him. I mean, sure, birthday parties are usually more fun than this party has been. But that's not really the point of a birthday party. The point is to build friendship.

Ken: But Rita, the whole point of friendship is to have fun. I used to really enjoy hanging out with Dale. Lately—not just at this party—he's been such a drag.

DOI: 10.4324/9781003238393-13

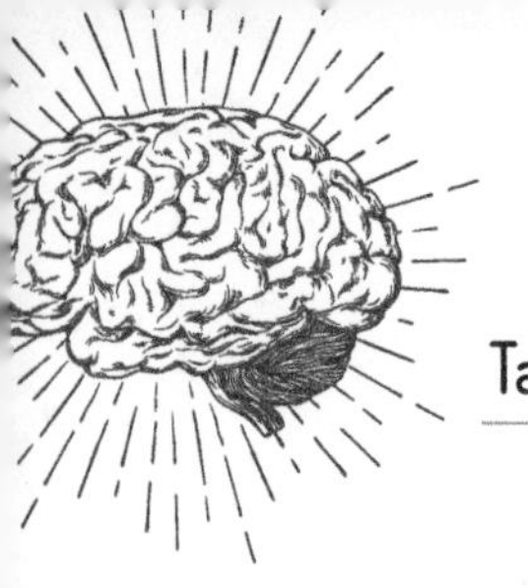

> **Rita:** Well, duh, that's because of his parents' divorce. It's been hard on him. I admit he hasn't been much fun lately. But I never liked him just for the fun times. I like him for who he is. He's a really good person.
>
> **Ken:** So was Mahatma Gandhi. That doesn't mean I would have wanted to be friends with him.
>
> **Rita:** Are you kidding? It would have been such an honor to be friends with Gandhi! Ken, you don't understand friendship at all. You're just using people to enjoy yourself.
>
> **Ken:** Life is all about trying to enjoy yourself—not just for me, but for everyone. I don't mind when other people enjoy me. So, why should they mind when I enjoy them? Go ahead, Rita, get a piece of cake and try to hit me. I think a big food fight is just what this party needs.

Stop for a moment to think about the two or three people you regard as your best friends. Who are they? How did you come to be friends? Why do you like them? Imagine that all of your best friends suddenly decided to move someplace far away, where there is no cellular communication. How would their absence affect you? Could you replace them without permanent damage? Or would the damage be permanent, like losing an arm or a leg?

What makes friendship such an important part of human life? Philosophers have pondered this question throughout history. Two ancient Greeks, Aristotle and Epicurus, developed opposing answers that set the stage for the ongoing debate. According to Aristotle, friendship is *intrinsically valuable*; according to Epicurus, it is *instrumentally valuable.* What exactly does this difference mean? This chapter will examine each answer in turn.

According to Aristotle, a true friend is "another self" who is lovable for their own sake. In other words, people love their friends regardless of any benefit the friends might happen to bring. This makes friendship different from almost everything else in life. Consider ice cream. Do you love ice cream for its own sake or because of the taste sensation it brings to you? Suppose ice cream suddenly stopped tasting good. Would you still love it? Of course not. Its only value lies in its ability to please you. The same is true of all human possessions—clothes, cars, houses, phones. People love these objects for how well they serve their purposes.

Aristotle insisted that true friends are not at all like possessions. People do not acquire a friend for a certain purpose, the way they might acquire a pair of cleats for soccer practice. Instead, they admire others for certain qualities they have. For example, someone might admire Mahatma Gandhi for his kindness and courage. It's not that they are hoping that he will be kind *to them* or brave *for them.* It's more like admiring a beautiful sculpture in an art museum; they are awed. As Gandhi's friend, they would celebrate his existence. He would inspire them to be courageous and kind like him. The closer their friendship became, Aristotle says, the more they would begin to feel like "a single soul inhabiting two bodies." To lose him would be devastating.

Of course, not many people are as virtuous as Gandhi. Most friends may seem rather ordinary by comparison. So, it may feel strange to admire friends like works of art. But at the same time, people don't become friends with just anyone at random. Something attracts certain people together and repels them from others. In this chapter's dialogue, Rita says she thinks Dale is a good person, and she likes him for who he is. Perhaps Dale has a sharp sense of humor, a gentle heart, a love of music, or an insightful outlook on life. She wants to be around him because she sees those things as virtues that she would like to develop and share. Rita will stick with Dale and support him through tough times because she stands for the same main values he does.

A **virtue** is a strength or area of personal excellence.

The Aristotelian Argument **FOR** the Intrinsic Value of Friendship

1. True friendship is the sharing of virtues.
2. The sharing of virtues is valuable in itself.
3. Whatever is valuable in itself is intrinsically valuable.
4. Therefore, true friendship is intrinsically valuable.

Aristotle did not hold that all friendships should be virtuous. He acknowledged that some friendships are formed for utility or pleasure. These relationships arise through school, business, or hobbies and exist for a specific purpose—for people to share notes, exchange goods, or compete with each other. Once the purpose is accomplished, the relationship ends. At the same time, Aristotle insisted that the highest form of friendship—true friendship—is pursued for its own sake, not for any other purpose. He wrote, "for without friends, no one would choose to live, though he had all other goods." Think about that: If you had wealth, wisdom, fame, beauty, and health, but no friends, could you be happy? Probably not. For Aristotle, this proves that true friendship is not the means to some further good, like in the case of a classmate, business partnership, or teammate. Rather, true friendship is a good of itself, for its own sake.

Aristotle

Epicurus disagreed. His departure began with skepticism toward Aristotle's notion of virtue. Think about some virtues—kindness, courage, sense of humor, gentleness, talent, insight. Are they really valuable for their own sake? Epicurus thought not. He argued that the reason people admire kindness is because it brings them pleasure. For example, a kind friend will give another person a gift on their birthday. Likewise, a courageous friend might encourage another person to ask someone to the dance. People enjoy receiving gifts and going to dances, and life is all about pursuing enjoyable things. So, in Epicurus's view, pleasure is the only real "virtue."

Epicurus wrote, "Pleasure is our first and kindred good. It is the starting point of every choice and of every aversion, and we always come back to it, inasmuch as we make feeling the rule for judging every good thing." If pleasure is the only thing with intrinsic value, it follows that friendship has instrumental value. According to this view, the sole purpose of friendship is to bring pleasure. Epicurus wrote, "A wise man chooses a happy and flexible friend." A friendship that fails to bring pleasure should be terminated.

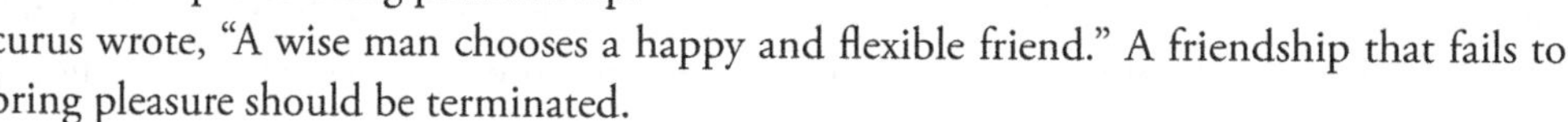

Epicurus

This may sound rather harsh at first. In the dialogue, Ken seems ready to abandon Dale for not being fun. Ken seems cold, a person who doesn't deserve any friends. But perhaps Ken's views are defensible with regard to two important features of the Epicurean view. First of all, Epicureans are in favor of promoting pleasure *in the long run*, not instant gratification. Epicurus wrote:

> When we say, then, that pleasure is the ultimate end, we do not mean prodigal or sensual pleasures, as ignorant or prejudiced people do. By pleasure we mean the absence of pain in the body and the absence of trouble in the soul. An unbroken succession of drinking, revelry, sexual lust, or luxurious delicacies will not produce an enjoyable life. Rather, an enjoyable life is the product of sober reasoning, wise choice, and banishing beliefs that lead to trouble.

Epicureans are against cheap thrills because they know that the immediate pleasure such things bring are far outweighed by the pain they cause in the end. They recommend reasoning carefully and making wise choices. For example, you may want to eat M&Ms for breakfast. But eating a healthy breakfast instead will enable you to win your school's 5K fun run, which you will enjoy much more. So, it would be consistent for Ken to stick with

Dale through the tough times provided the tough times don't change Dale into someone who has forgotten how to enjoy life.

Secondly, an Epicurean might point out that people often hold onto friendships they shouldn't. The emphasis on "sticking together through thick and thin" ignores the fact that relationships can become toxic. Sometimes people change in ways that are no longer compatible. Perhaps Dale used to love outdoor sports like Ken but has grown to prefer reading and building models. Because Ken still loves outdoor sports, it is unlikely that Ken and Dale are going to enjoy spending time together anymore. They should go their separate ways and not feel bad about it. If they try to force the continuation of their friendship, they will inevitably fight and come to hate each other. Because hatred is not pleasant, it is better to move on and find new friends.

Although the Epicurean view of friendship may seem ruthless, it may be more realistic than the Aristotelian view. Epicurus agreed with Aristotle about the importance of friendship. He wrote, "Of all the things which wisdom provides to make us entirely happy, much the greatest is the possession of friendship." Notice the word *possession* here. Although Aristotle denied that friends are like possessions, Epicurus insisted that they are like possessions—friends should be acquired to serve the goal of enjoying life.

The Epicurean Argument **FOR** the Instrumental Value of Friendship

1. True friendship leads to pleasure.
2. Pleasure is the only ultimate value.
3. Whatever leads to the only ultimate value is instrumentally valuable.
4. Therefore, true friendship is instrumentally valuable.

Thought Experiment

Imagine you have access to other people's thoughts and life experiences through some form of telepathy. You therefore find out that a friend of yours has a disease, Disease D, although they would never tell anyone this. You also know that there is a cure to the disease, Remedy X. Remedy X is very valuable, and you previously worked to acquire a bottle of it because you thought that you might someday contract Disease D. Your friend has been unable to get Remedy X. Do you find a way to secretly give them your bottle?

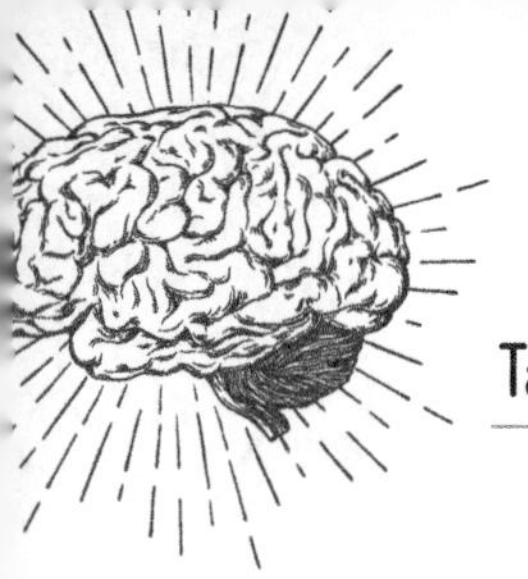

Thought Experiment, continued

The two conceptions of friendship examined in this chapter give different answers. If you subscribe to Aristotle's intrinsic view, then you probably would give your friend the bottle. Their well-being is as important as your own because you share the same values. Aristotle's commitment to virtue implies that he is willing to sacrifice himself. Things look different, however, from Epicurus's instrumental view of friendship. You may not give your friend the bottle because you can keep their friendship as long as they live and keep the bottle in case you need it. It seems nothing could ever prompt Epicurus to sacrifice himself.

Personal Statement

You may be thinking that Aristotle's view seems too demanding, while Epicurus's view seems inhumane. Is there some way to strike a compromise between these two extremes? We believe there is.

What if we told you there may be a way to care about friends in an instrumental way that is indistinguishable from the intrinsic way? Suppose Epicurus is correct that the primary goal of friendship is to bring pleasure to the individual, but Aristotle is correct that true friends must be treated as intrinsically valuable. Think about it like this: Would you continue to be friends with someone if you knew they didn't care about you for your own sake, but were just using you for their own pleasure? Probably not. Thus, it is important to treat your friends as though they are valuable in themselves, even if they are not. If you treat your friends as nothing but a means to your pleasure, then you will have fewer friends, and therefore less pleasure.

People need friends in order to gain pleasure. But the only way to gain friends is to treat them as valuable in themselves. So treating people as valuable in themselves helps to achieve the subgoal of having friends, which, in turn, helps to achieve the ultimate goal of having pleasure. We therefore conclude that the best way to enjoy life is to give friendship this *pseudointrinsic value*.

The two authors of this chapter have discussed this together. We know that we value each other in this pseudointrinsic way. Yet we are good friends and have a lot of fun together. So—who knows?—maybe we are right!

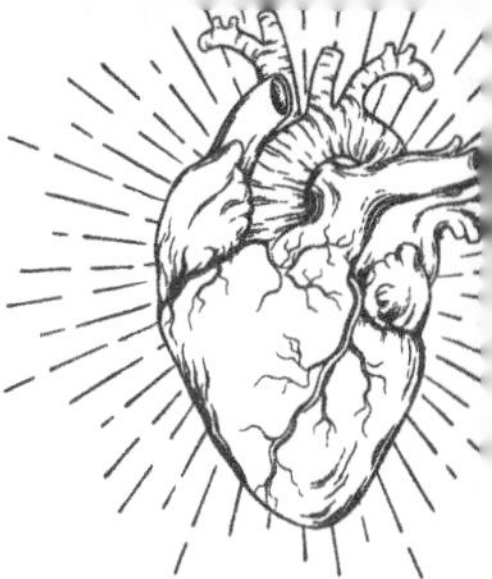

Discussion Questions

1. Would you keep your current friendships if you learned your friends' motives were only to satisfy their own pleasure? Assume they will continue to act in the same way they always have.
2. If your friend had no lunch, and you were able to give them part of yours, would you do it? What would your reasons be? Do you care about their hunger, or would you share because you expect them to return the favor in some way?
3. Who do you agree with most—Aristotle or Epicurus? Why? If you are undecided, what problems do you have with each, and what would you need to know to take a position?
4. Could you live a happy life without friends? If you believe that friends are only instruments of pleasure, in theory, couldn't you get your pleasures from another source to achieve the same result?
5. Consider the Thought Experiment section of this chapter. What would you do if you had a bottle of Remedy X?

Classroom Activities

1. Write a quiz about yourself for everyone in the class to take. The questions should address who you are personally. Consider your classmates' answers. Who knows you best? Who do you know best? Who would you like to know better? Discuss to what extent knowledge is important for friendship.
2. Create a class word cloud by brainstorming words that come to mind when you think of friendship. Discuss what you think the word cloud reveals.

References

Aristotle. (2016). *Nicomachean ethics* (W. D. Ross, Trans.). http://classics.mit.edu/Aristotle/metaphysics.html (Original worked published 350 BCE)

Epicurus. (n.d.) *Letter to Menoeceus* (R. D. Hicks, Trans.). http://classics.mit.edu/Epicurus/menoec.html

Chapter 10

Is It Wrong to Be Selfish?

by
Tristan Hansen

[Philip meets Alex outside after school, and they begin walking home.]

Alex: Did you hear about what happened to Sam last night?

Philip: Yeah, I heard. His house caught on fire, right?

Alex: Right. No one was hurt. But all of Sam's stuff—his clothes, his laptop, everything—was destroyed, just like that. And his family doesn't have insurance.

Philip: Bummer.

Alex: Yeah. A bunch of us were thinking about chipping in some cash to help Sam out.

Philip: Uh . . . you mean like you're going to give him your own money?

Alex: Exactly—we figure it's the least we could do. Are you in?

Philip: Me? Nope. I'm saving up for a ski trip.

Alex: Come on, dude. Don't be so selfish!

Philip: Hey—there's nothing wrong with being selfish to a reasonable degree! I'm not going to spend my hard-earned money on someone I don't even like. You have to admit Sam's not the nicest guy in the world. In fact, he's pretty freaking rude.

 DOI: 10.4324/9781003238393-14

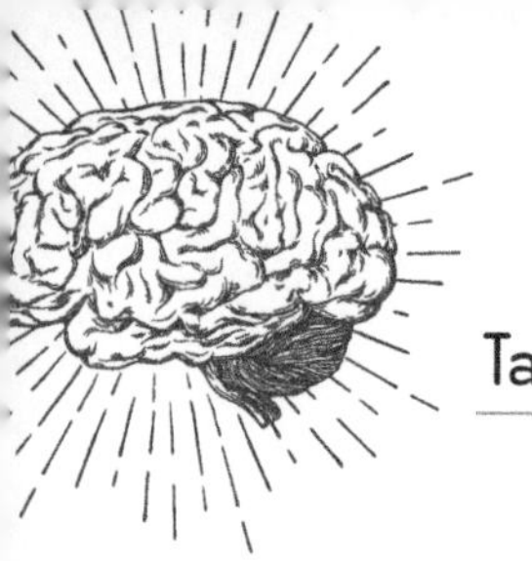

Altruism is when someone selflessly helps others.

Alex: Well, if we help him out, he may actually learn to be nice to us, and vice versa.

Philip: Look, if *you* want to give him money, feel free, but keep me out of it. Don't get me wrong—I feel bad for his family and everything. But I've got to do what's in my best interest.

Alex: I bet you would help him if he was a friend of yours.

Philip: Probably. It would be in my best interest to help a friend. But Sam isn't my friend—or yours either.

Alex: My point is that he could be if we reach out. Now's our chance.

Philip: I don't know, man . . . I'll have to think about it.

People are often taught the value of altruism in society: that they should serve and concern themselves with others. Society praises those who are willing to sacrifice themselves to help people in need. The idea of prioritizing oneself over others is usually frowned upon. However, some philosophers argue that selfishness is a virtue.

Twentieth-century philosopher Ayn Rand made her mark in the world of literature with several bestselling novels. Among them was *Atlas Shrugged,* which features the character John Galt, who believes that every human being has the right to use their mind solely for themselves. John Galt illustrates Rand's philosophical theory, which she called *objectivism.* This theory is extremely controversial because it contradicts the commitment to helping others that society has come to value so deeply. Objectivism prioritizes rational self-interest and views altruism as an evil. Despite the opposition she faced, Rand adamantly proclaimed that selfishness is a virtue.

Ayn Rand

To be virtuous, one does not need to be, in Rand's words, "a sacrificial animal." People can and should be selfish. In fact, human beings are unlikely to achieve maximum success in life if they primarily prioritize the needs of others over themselves. For example, in *Atlas Shrugged,* John Galt is a brilliant inventor who organizes a successful strike against his company when it tries to enforce altruistic policies. People must focus on their own self-interest in order to reach their highest potential. Rand wrote, "Man is entitled to his own happiness and must achieve it himself." In fact, she argued that it is immoral to make someone suffer so that others can benefit. Selfishness is not wrong. On the contrary, it is virtuous, because when individuals realize their highest potential, society as a whole does, too.

Rand's Argument *FOR* Selfishness

1. It is a virtue to prioritize one's own happiness through rational means.
2. When people act selfishly, they prioritize their own happiness.
3. When people act selfishly, they act rationally.
4. Therefore, selfishness is a virtue.

One might object that the whole idea of virtue is to be morally good, and there is nothing morally good about prioritizing oneself over others. People admire those who help others selflessly, regardless of the cost. How can society realize its highest potential when some people's needs are not being met? For example, suppose John Galt invents an amazing new kind of car. Can society celebrate this new car while doing nothing to help the homeless people on the streets? If John Galt's new car runs over one of these homeless people, should society pretend not to notice and leave them to die?

Rand might reply that she is not advocating hurting other people. Being selfish does not imply deliberate harm to anyone. Furthermore, selfish people may still help others, provided it is in their own best interest as well. In other words, it is possible for other people to benefit from the rational selfishness that an individual may exhibit. For example, suppose you refuse to donate your money to a charitable foundation because you are saving up to buy a birthday gift for your mother. In this situation, you're being selfish by not giving your money to the foundation, but someone else (your mother) is going to benefit from it. Full-blown, unrestrained selfishness can be irrational. Rand would not consider it a virtue. Her contention was that rational selfishness is a virtue.

Thought Experiment

Imagine you live in the year 3020. A new technology, the Experience Machine, has been developed. Similar to virtual reality, this machine goes over your head and eyes and creates a simulation for you. However, this technology is highly advanced; your brain is completely convinced that what you're experiencing is real. The system is set up so that you could live out your life hooked up to this machine, and the simulations would provide you with everything you could possibly want. However, you would not be contributing anything to your society. While you lived in this perfect world, other people outside the simulation, including your family, would be forced to face gritty reality.

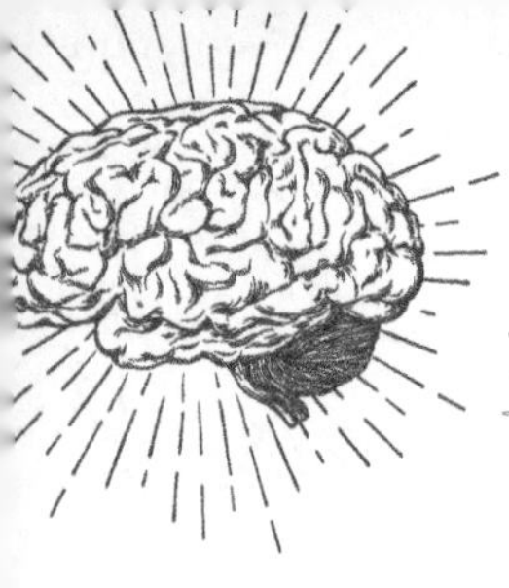

Thought Experiment, continued

Would you want to live your life hooked up to this machine? If yes, then perhaps Rand is right. If not, then it seems there's more to life than selfishness. But what?

C. S. Lewis gave a suggestion about why the selfish life is not the best life. Lewis was an influential 20th-century author and philosopher who wrote many celebrated works of literature, including the *Chronicles of Narnia*. The lead character of this series is Aslan, a talking lion, who promotes the idea of loving one's fellow creatures. In the story, Aslan decides to save a boy named Edmund, who betrayed him earlier in the story. When Edmund is about to be murdered by the White Witch, Aslan insists that she kill Aslan instead. Aslan was able to put Edmund's past actions aside and focus on sacrificing himself for the common good. In this way, Lewis was the polar opposite of Rand. He did not believe selfishness was something to be proud of. Instead, he encouraged people to be willing to sacrifice themselves and support others in any situation.

Lewis defined four different kinds of love:

- *Storge*, which is affection;
- *Eros*, which is romantic passion;
- *Philia*, which is friendship; and
- *Agape*, which is charity.

Lewis argued that Agape is the highest form of love. It is how God loves human beings: selflessly and unconditionally.

Altruism is difficult to achieve because it usually involves some sort of self-sacrifice. For example, within the Narnia series, Mr. Tumnus is arrested and turned to stone by the White Witch for protecting Lucy Pevensie. Despite hardly knowing Tumnus, Lucy feels guilty for his suffering. She becomes determined to save him regardless of the danger she could face. Likewise, Lewis argued that people should help others regardless of how they feel about them:

> The rule for all of us is perfectly simple. Do not waste time bothering whether you "love" your neighbor; act as if you did. As soon as we do this we find one of the great secrets. When you are behaving as if you loved someone, you will presently come to love him. If you injure someone you

> dislike, you will find yourself disliking him more. If you do him a good turn, you will find yourself disliking him less.

Lewis argued that if people ignore or hurt those they hate, their hatred will only become stronger. By helping others, over time, they can learn to like and even love others, who in turn, may reciprocate that feeling. In other words, altruism contributes to a life of love, which is better than a life of selfishness.

Lewis's Argument *AGAINST* Selfishness

1. Altruism brings about a life of love.
2. A life of love is better than a selfish life.
3. Therefore, altruism is better than selfishness.

Someone might object that people don't change from hate to love as easily as Lewis suggests. People tend to hold fast to their opinions of others and are unlikely to be open-minded enough to like someone whom they once hated. For example, due to ingrained racist beliefs, a person may adamantly refuse to lend money to someone of a different race regardless of how altruistic or kind that other person may be. Furthermore, people will likely take advantage of altruistic people, making them suffer. A selfish person may fake feeling love for an altruistic person in order to gain benefits. If these flaws are embedded in human nature, then Lewis's proposal for a life of love seems unrealistic.

Lewis might respond, however, that human nature is not set in stone. Selfish people may not at first be willing to reciprocate the altruism that someone else shows them. However, if the altruistic individual remains committed and consistent in their generous behavior, then it is likely that the selfish person will eventually feel the need to reciprocate it. After all, it is human nature to need each of the four forms of love Lewis outlined. In his view, people especially need Agape. Everyone wants to be liked and needs to be accepted. Eventually, even the most selfish people can learn to exhibit altruistic behavior.

Personal Statement

Throughout my life I have considered altruism to be a positive trait for someone to exhibit. In my view, Rand is incorrect to say that altruism is an evil and shouldn't be valued. In fact, I believe it is a pivotal part of a healthy society.

I myself have come to like someone I once hated through altruism. For the first 17 years of my life, I considered my brother to be an immature and mean-spirited individual. He would relentlessly tease me or exclude me from activities. We seemed to be polar opposites who were destined to hate each other forever. However, as my brother matured, he began making efforts to mend our broken bond. He started talking to me more and including me in discussions. Although I was hesitant and cautious at first, I soon realized

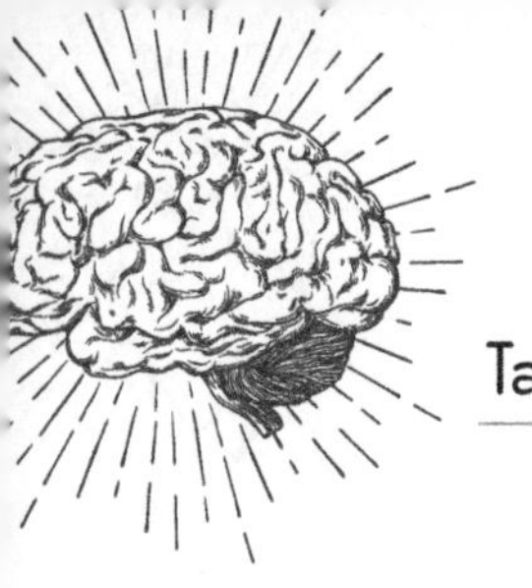

his intentions were pure. As we interacted, we began to realize that we had more in common than we thought, and our bond grew strong. Due to my brother's altruistic behavior, he has become my closest friend.

However, I agree with Rand that a certain amount of rational selfishness is crucial for a person to function and be happy. People must be careful not to have so much concern for others that they neglect their own needs. I will gladly sacrifice my time and effort to help others, as long as their needs are reasonable. For example, I'm willing to give money to a homeless person as long as I have the excess funds to do so. However, I will not give away the money I have if I know I will need it to pay my debts. I believe in having rational self-interest along with altruism.

Discussion Questions

1. Do you think helping out a friend can be altruistic, or do you think it is always in your own best interest?
2. Do you think it is possible for someone to exhibit both altruism and selfishness at the same time?
3. Between altruism and selfishness, which behavior do you consider to be the most beneficial to an individual's happiness?
4. Can self-sacrificial actions still be considered altruistic if they were performed for selfish reasons?
5. Think of a favorite book or movie that illustrates your view about love and selfishness.

Classroom Activities

1. Volunteer for a community service activity, such as raising money through a bake sale or car wash, or picking up trash at a nearby park. Discuss who benefitted from this activity and how.
2. Keep a diary for a week noting three kind things you did each day. At the end of the week review your diary. Write and share a report on whether you are an egoist or an altruist.

References

Atlas Society. (2013). *Ayn Rand Mike Wallace interview (Part 1) 1959*. YouTube. https://www.youtube.com/watch?v=Fi9DVLm_6XA

CSLewisDoodle. (2018). *The four loves ('Agape' or 'God's love') by C.S. Lewis doodle*. YouTube. https://www.youtube.com/watch?v=gaVaGGpeQKM

Lewis, C. S. (2015). *Mere Christianity*. Macmillan. (Original work published 1960)

Chapter 11

Is It Wrong to Eat Meat?

by
Maria Genova

[Cecil and Lionel are out with their families at the new restaurant in town.]

Cecil: There are a lot of weird things on this menu. What are you going to order, Lionel?

Lionel: I was thinking about trying the venison.

Cecil: Venison? What's that?

Lionel: It's meat that comes from deer. It's good! You should try it.

Cecil: You mean people eat deer? Ew . . . I would never!

Lionel: Some people do, though. Lots of different cultures eat different meats. Did you know that a common dish in Peru is guinea pig? You only consider it normal to eat beef and pork because that's what you were raised on.

Cecil: I would never eat a guinea pig! I had one as a pet when I was little. Maybe we shouldn't eat deer either. They're so cute!

Lionel: And maybe we shouldn't eat beef, then. Cows are pretty cute.

Cecil: Maybe . . .

Humans have a complex relationship with animals, having historically relied on them for survival. This reliance has been mostly for food; however, animals have been used for other

DOI: 10.4324/9781003238393-15

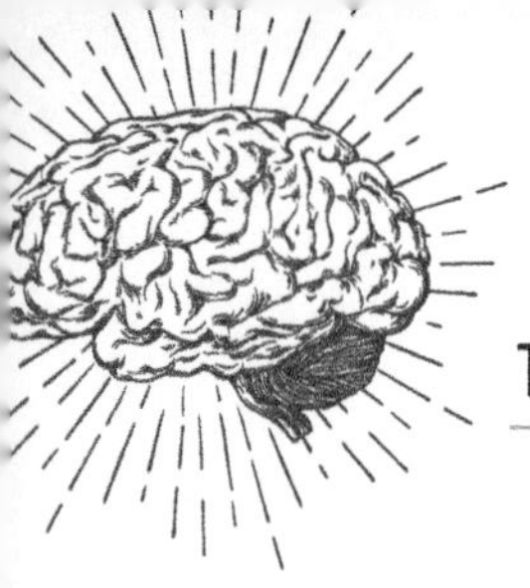

purposes as well, such as for the production of clothing and tools. As the human species has grown and advanced, people's relationship with animals has changed. For instance, humans now have means of manufacturing fabric for clothing rather than using the skins of animals. Likewise, animal fats are no longer necessary to create soaps or fuel lamps. In fact it is possible to live without the use of any animal products at all. This has led philosophers to consider whether or not it is ethical to continue to use them.

Speciesism: Favoring the interest of one's own species over the interests of others; discriminating based on species membership.

It is fairly easy to argue against inessential items like fur coats and leather purses. After all, the life of an animal seems more important than a fashion statement. But what about food? With advanced farming methods and meat substitutes, humans do not have to rely on meat in order to meet their dietary needs. Still, eating affordable food that people like is pretty important to human happiness. Is it wrong to eat meat?

One of the most influential arguments for abstaining from eating meat comes from Peter Singer, an Australian philosopher who is credited with starting the modern animal rights movement. Singer pointed out that people have long given moral consideration to members of the human community. But why? It's because people sympathize with other beings like them. When a person sees other people suffer, they feel for them; they feel it is wrong to make someone suffer. It would not be wrong to kick a rock, as rocks do not have the capacity to feel pain. However, it would be wrong to kick another human, as they would be hurt by this action. Clearly moral consideration is based on capacity for suffering: When deciding whether an action is right or wrong, people must take into account whether it increases the total amount of pain in the world.

Singer believed that his case for animal rights followed directly from the moral theory known as utilitarianism. This theory holds that actions that promote the most overall happiness should be favored. Conversely, actions that promote unhappiness are less desirable. Singer acknowledged that humans have historically acted as though the pain of animals simply doesn't count. Perhaps this was through sheer necessity, when humans were struggling to survive and had few other reliable sources of food. But the vast majority of human beings today no longer have that excuse. For people to discount animal pain as though it isn't as important as human pain is sheer bias. Singer called this bias "speciesism" and compared it to racism or sexism.

To better understand how speciesism impacts humans' attitude toward animals, consider the following thought experiment. Imagine that you are reincarnated as a herring. As a herring, you have several natural predators, including salmon. Naturally, you want to survive, and it is in your best interest to avoid being eaten by salmon. Next, imagine that you are reincarnated as a salmon. As a salmon, you also want to survive and avoid suffering. So, it is in your best interest to eat your prey, the herring. In both of your lives, as a herring and as a salmon, you want your own needs to be prioritized. As a herring, you might say that your desire to not be eaten is more important than the salmon's desire to eat you. However, as a salmon, you would most likely say that your need to eat is more important. As both a salmon and a herring, you would want your own desire not to suffer to be taken into account. It would be unfair to prioritize one species' interests over the others. Singer's argument for speciesism works much the same way. People need to recog-

nize that all animals want to avoid suffering. It would be unfair and biased to say that the interests of any one species are more important than all others.

Singer argued that there is no reason to believe human pain and suffering are any more important than animal pain and suffering. Someone might object that animals don't understand their suffering the way humans do, which makes their suffering less important. But Singer would not be moved by this objection. After all, there are humans with mental disabilities who do not fully understand their suffering. Yet they are still worthy of moral consideration, simply due to their membership in the human community. Singer contended that animals and humans are equally worthy of moral consideration. One cannot base moral consideration on understanding. All beings with the capacity to suffer have an equal interest in avoiding suffering, whether they understand it or not. Therefore, it is wrong to cause animals to suffer.

Moral omnivorism: The position that meat and other animal food products can be consumed ethically.

Singer's Argument *AGAINST* Eating Meat

1. Humans have a moral responsibility to minimize pain in the world.
2. The meat industry causes pain in the world by making animals suffer.
3. Therefore, humans have a responsibility to minimize the meat industry.

One response to Singer's argument comes from the contemporary philosopher Seungbae Park, who argued for a position of *moral omnivorism*. Park adopted Singer's tenet that "all animals are equal" and used it to defend his own claim that humans are justified in eating meat. Park began by pointing toward other omnivores' behavior in the wild. Baboons and bears, for example, prefer to eat meat even though they are capable of surviving without it. If people truly want to embrace the tenet that all animals are equal, then they need to apply it to baboons and bears as well as humans. Humans would never punish a bear or a baboon for eating meat, so they shouldn't punish a human for eating meat either. Animals gladly eat other animals. It would be unfair to hold humans to a higher standard. Therefore, humans should not be condemned for eating the meat of animals.

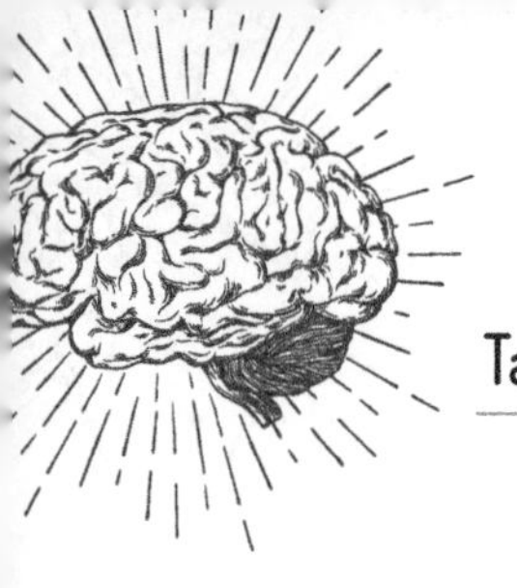

Like Singer, Park was concerned about using suffering as a standard for judging human actions. He argued that because omnivores prefer to eat meat, giving meat up constitutes suffering. It is in the interest of all living beings to avoid suffering. In order to maintain that "all animals are equal," people must grant that the human interest in avoiding suffering is the same as that of other animals. It discriminates against humans to claim that human suffering caused by not eating meat is less important than the suffering of animals. Therefore, humans should not be required to give up meat.

Park's Argument *FOR* Eating Meat

1. It is not wrong for animals to kill other animals for food.
2. Humans and animals should be held to the same standard.
3. Therefore, it is not wrong for humans to kill animals for food.

Park granted, however, that there are both ethical and unethical ways for humans to consume meat. He cited factory farming as a method of producing meat that violates the tenet that all animals are equal. Livestock must be raised in humane conditions and provided the opportunity to live as long as they would have in the wild. The only time humans would cause the animals suffering, according to this alternative, is at the time of their deaths.

Park argued that humans are justified in eating meat and urged them to do so morally. Although encouraging humans to reduce animal suffering, he granted that this may be difficult. Human action will always interfere with animals' lives. For instance, driving cars harms animals in many ways. The creation of highways and roads disrupts natural habitats, cutting animals off from food sources and interrupting migration—not to mention that humans often accidently kill animals with their cars. Park acknowledged that it would be too difficult for most people to give up driving cars. Giving up cars for the sake of animals would be going above and beyond moral duty. This reasoning might be extended to ethical farming methods, which are more costly than the alternative and, therefore, not an option for some people. For instance, it may be necessary for a family to spend money on medicine rather than buying ethically farmed meat. In the end, Park promoted ethical meat consumption while allowing that this option is not a realistic for everyone.

The cases for and against eating meat as presented by Park and Singer can be extended further to the use of animal products in general. Humans consume not only the meat of animals, but also animal products, such as milk, eggs, and honey. Humans use animal skins and furs in the production of clothing and tools. And what about medical testing? Here, the relationship between humans and animals is even further complicated, as humans intentionally cause suffering to tested animals, but that testing can result in improving or even saving human lives. The question of whether or not it is wrong for humans to eat meat is just one of many questions surrounding humans' relationship with animals.

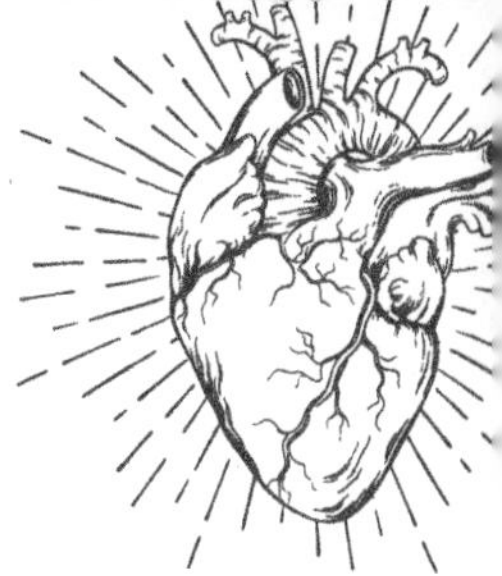

Personal Statement

In my personal life, I have come to prefer food sources other than meat. When I do eat meat, I make an effort to find locally raised, humane meat. I also make an effort to eat meat that can be farmed sustainably, like poultry and fish. Raising these animals has much less environmental impact than does raising cows and pigs. Although I take measures to reduce my own consumption of meat, I remain cognizant that cultural, economic, or health concerns may block this option for others.

Discussion Questions

1. Do you prefer to eat meat? If so, is this because you think meat is better than other foods or because you're used to it? Do you feel giving up meat would constitute suffering for you? Why or why not?
2. What do you think would happen if everyone in the world became vegetarian overnight? Would the new vegetarian world be better or worse than the current omnivore world?
3. Park argued that all animals are equal. Do you agree? Even mosquitos? Should the needs of some animals be prioritized over the needs of others, and on what basis?
4. Singer argued that animal suffering should be avoided at all costs. Should this claim apply in cases where animal suffering leads to human betterment, such as animal testing for medical technologies?
5. Is there really no difference between human and animal omnivorism, as Park argued, or does the ability to reason give humans an ethical responsibility that nonhumans don't have?

Classroom Activities

1. Spend a week as a vegetarian or, if you are already a vegetarian, as a vegan. (If you are already a vegan, give up one of your guilty pleasures.) At the end of the week share your experiences and thoughts about the sacrifice.
2. Estimate how many cows the class will eat this year. Calculate how much methane the class will be responsible for through this alone.

References

Park, S. (2017). Moral vegetarianism vs. moral omnivorism. *Human Affairs, 27*(3), 289–300. https://doi.org/10.1515/humaff-2017-0024

Singer, P. (2009). *Animal liberation: The definitive classic of the animal movement* (Updated ed.). HarperCollins.

Chapter 12

What Do People Owe to the Environment?

by
Oliver Golias

[Kamala and Xander are sitting across from each other in study hall.]

Xander: Kamala, what's going on with your eyes? They look so dark and droopy!

Kamala: Thanks, Xander, very flattering. I haven't been able to sleep the past couple days.

Xander: Whoa, sorry, I didn't know. What's going on?

Kamala: Well, it all started last week when my neighbor began biking to his job. I asked him why he'd do that when it's so cold outside, and he said it was to save the planet.

Xander: Save the planet? Like climate change stuff? What does that have to do with your sleep?

Kamala: I thought about how I should be saving the planet, too! He told me a little about climate change, and I've been up every night reading reports and articles because I want to help.

Xander: Okay, but it looks like you may be working yourself a little too hard. I mean it's cool that you want to learn about that stuff, but you need to rest some, too.

DOI: 10.4324/9781003238393-16

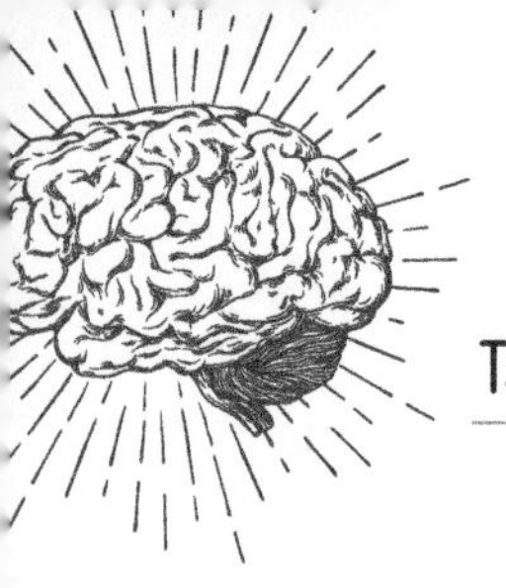

Kamala: That's the thing. I need to learn everything I can about this because I don't want to be guilty of making things worse! If I know everything about climate change, I can help, but if not, who knows how I might be hurting the environment?

Xander: Slow down, Kamala! I see what you mean, but you still deserve a break, right? So what if you mess up a little? Yeah, you might cause harm, but it's not like you meant to. It's like when Chauncy dropped that water balloon off the roof and it sprayed water on everyone below. He didn't know!

Kamala: That's kind of my point, though, Xander. He should have made sure no one was around if he really wanted to drop that balloon. I need to make sure nothing I do will hurt the planet because ignorance is not an excuse!

Xander: Alright, dude, just get some sleep. Yeah, you should ride your bike or whatever, but I think you need as much help as the planet right now.

Climate change is already creating problems that were predicted in the past: rising sea levels, shrinking glaciers, changes in the seasons, and altered harvests due to warming. If nothing is done, these problems will continue to worsen, eventually threatening life on Earth. Because human behavior affects climate change, which in turn affects people, climate change is a moral issue.

The philosophical community is trying to sort out what humans owe to the environment. In the dialogue, Xander asks Kamala if people must sacrifice their quality of life to save the planet. She presents two related types of responsibility: becoming informed about the problem and taking steps to avoid making the problem worse. There are two main positions on these responsibilities. Following Judith Jarvis Thomson, I'll call them the *Minimally Decent Samaritan* and the *Splendid Samaritan*.

Thomson is a Minimally Decent Samaritan. According to her view, people are only responsible for limiting harm, and they are not required to go out of their way to do this. Although the story of the Good Samaritan is moving, Thomson saw the Good Samaritan's actions as unnecessary. Doing nothing would be wrong, but he was not morally obligated to do so much. The Good Samaritan was actually a Splendid Samaritan in her view. The Minimally Decent Samaritan would be more likely to call the police and let them tend to the situation. He would acknowledge the problem without sacrificing his own quality of life to help.

In the dialogue, Kamala is first concerned about informing herself. Ignorance is tough because, in order to address it, a person has to know what they don't know! When a person is really not aware that they are lacking important information, they are *unwittingly ignorant.* To eliminate this excuse, activists have been raising consciousness about the environmental crisis. It is covered on the news and taught in science classes at schools, so there probably are not many people out there who are unwittingly ignorant of it anymore.

Even given a general awareness of the environmental crisis, however, a person might find themselves lacking important information. For example, suppose you don't know whether a certain type of container is recyclable. You keep throwing this type of container in the recycle bin, aware that you may be contaminating the bin with unrecyclable material. You could easily find out what you are supposed to do with this type of container, but you don't. This is called *witting ignorance*. The Minimally Decent Samaritan view holds that people are responsible for remedying their witting ignorance. Many philosophers agree that humans' right to life includes "the right to live well." With this in mind, educating oneself is necessary for minimal decency, but not to the point of losing sleep. As rights apply to everyone, people must respect their own right to live well.

Carbon footprint: The total amount of damaging gas a person is responsible for emitting through the use of products and services that burn fossil fuels.

Kamala is also concerned about reducing her carbon footprint. Although it may seem straightforward to change her lifestyle after finding out what needs to be done, it isn't so easy. How far out of her way is she willing to go? It is tempting not to go very far, especially because one person alone can't solve the problem. Massive cooperation will be necessary to achieve significant improvement. This fact has prompted some philosophers to ask whether every person should take responsibility for organizing a collection of people to reduce the overall carbon footprint.

Each person must cut down on their carbon footprint because every footprint makes a negative impact on the environment. With that said, cutting back really is the minimally decent thing to do—but to what extent? The threshold for minimal decency varies among individuals. Some people are able to afford solar panels for their houses, and others are not. It is up to each person to honestly assess what they can afford.

Thomson's position is minimally decent because it establishes the need for a threshold. Going past this threshold is not wrong, of course, as long as it is not imposed on others, but everyone is expected to do their part. To respond to climate change, the Minimally Decent Samaritan does what must be done, but not necessarily more, out of respect for the quality of their own life.

The Good Samaritan by Rembrandt (1630). This painting depicts the Good Samaritan making arrangements with the innkeeper.

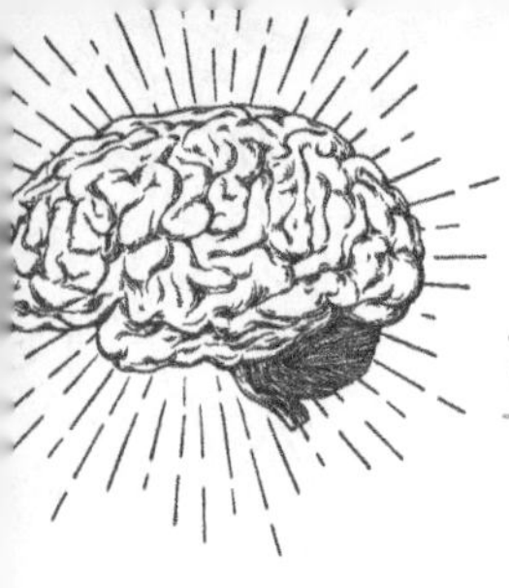

The Minimally Decent Samaritan Argument

1. No one is obligated to violate their own right to life.
2. Being required to make sacrifices for the environment violates one's right to life.
3. Therefore, no one is obligated to make sacrifices for the environment.

Although the Minimally Decent Samaritan is a fine basis for moral responsibility, many philosophers maintain that moral obligation to the environment goes beyond the minimum to the point of sacrifice. Does the environment have the right to demand that humans decrease their current quality of life to save it? Not exactly. But the Splendid Samaritan argues that future generations of humans do have this right. As the environmental crisis goes on, humans are damaging the future state of the world. To carry on without making sacrifices implies that future humans will be miserable or even killed. Whose rights are more important: the present generation's or the future generation's?

The Minimally Decent Samaritan wants to allow for "business as usual." Admittedly, it is not certain exactly how much damage this approach will do. It is certain, however, that business as usual will leave either the same amount or more harm than conservation. Tim Mulgan argued that this is enough reason to make sacrifices. Mulgan represents the Splendid Samaritan perspective: that conserving the environment is a moral obligation. When someone's rights are infringed, that person deserves compensation to some degree. Simply by participating in society, humans add to the environmental harm future generations will inherit. Because of this, society as a whole is obligated to compensate future generations, but the only method of compensation for this group is reducing the harm in the first place. Because future generations have not been born yet, there is nothing society can give them other than a future. Assuming that their rights are relevant, people are morally obligated to sacrifice some quality of life to protect that future.

Agreeing with Thomson that people must address their witting ignorance, Mulgan went further. Given the current generation's obligation to future generations, people need to go out of their way to get the information they need to make the right choices. For the Splendid Samaritan, it is not enough to address witting ignorance because every question that is answered leads to a new question. According to this view, it is one's moral duty to strive for expert knowledge on the environment.

Naturally, the Splendid Samaritan view also insists that each person must make sacrifices to avoid making the problem worse. Like the Good Samaritan, who paid the innkeeper to look after the injured man, people need to give up some luxuries. Presumably, the Good Samaritan did not pay the innkeeper his last dollar, but he paid his own hard-earned cash, which he could have used to buy himself a new hat.

Mulgan was careful to point out, however, that people can demand sacrifice only insofar as no further injustice is committed. For example, if the government made a law requiring everyone to ride a bicycle to work, this would give people living in cities an unfair advantage over rural dwellers. The sacrifices made for future generations have to be voluntary, or, if required by law, they have to be luxuries rather than necessities.

Unfortunately, the only way to eliminate one's carbon footprint is to withdraw from society. As this is an unreasonable expectation, it is understandable that individuals will continue to make carbon footprints. The Splendid Samaritan urges individuals to sacrifice as much as possible in the name of future generations. Because there is no option but to infringe on the rights of these generations, people must do what they can to compensate for that harm.

The Splendid Samaritan Argument

1. All those who are currently alive are damaging the planet.
2. Damaging the planet violates the rights of future generations.
3. When a person violates someone's rights, they are morally obligated to compensate them.
4. The only way to compensate future generations is to make sacrifices for the environment.
5. Therefore, all those who are currently alive are obligated to make sacrifices for the environment.

Personal Statement

In my view, the Splendid Samaritan makes the stronger case. Although minimal decency is a good standard of moral obligation in general, I believe climate change is a large enough issue for people to raise their usual moral standards. In most cases, the minimum would be simply acknowledging the situation and not intentionally increasing harm. If only that were enough to solve the problem! The environmental crisis is already severe enough that people have to be proactive. Business as usual is beginning to seem indecent, which means that society may need a new definition of minimum decency.

Cutting luxuries is a great start, provided that people recognize how many of the things they take for granted are actually luxuries. They should be riding bikes to work, buying eco-friendly lightbulbs, composting food waste, etc. But to make a real difference, governments must enforce restrictions, too. For example, governments could begin refining plastic products into fuel. Given the right technology and enough plastic, this could make a difference. There is room for debating possible injustices with governmental action, but there are still many laws that can be pushed for.

Many options that might seem bizarre and difficult at first could become comfortable over time. For instance, eating insects rather than meat would reduce emissions significantly. Approximately 3% of emissions in the United States are caused by livestock digestive processes. This does not even account for how the livestock's waste and food are managed, so shifting the burden of food production to insects would cause significant reductions. Short of that, eating meat less often or going vegetarian could help a lot.

Although the route of conserving the environment is strenuous, people can do it if they see the value of being a Splendid Samaritan.

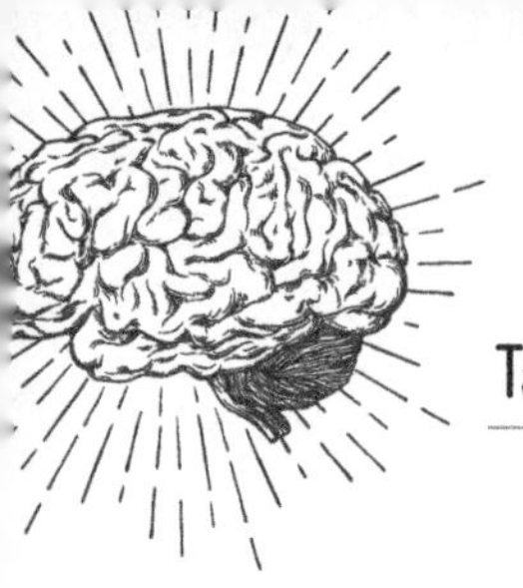

Discussion Questions

1. Is it necessary to change one's life to be morally justified in terms of climate change? Assuming it is necessary, should governments enforce laws to encourage citizens to do so?
2. What might a conservationist say to Kamala about her lack of sleep? Where is the threshold is in trying to overcome witting ignorance?
3. Because reducing emissions requires such a large group effort, is there much value in one person's effort? Is it better to direct your focus on reducing your own emissions or getting a group to join you?
4. What kind of things can you do to minimize your negative impact on the environment?

Classroom Activities

1. Brainstorm a list of things the class could do to reduce its footprint. Pick the most realistic and impactful thing. Create a system for keeping track of your individual efforts. At the end of the week, combine your data and celebrate your accomplishment.
2. Write a letter to your future grandchildren about the things you vow to do to compensate for damaging the environment. Put the letter in an envelope labeled, "Please open in 2080." Tuck the letter in your baby book or some other family keepsake that is liable to be kept safe and passed down.

References

King James Bible. (2017). King James Bible online. https://www.kingjamesbibleonline.org (Original work published 1769)

Mulgan, T. (2018). Answering to future people: Responsibility for climate change in a breaking world. *Journal of Applied Philosophy, 35*(3), 532–548. https://doi.org/10.1111/japp.12222

NASA. (2019). *The effects of climate change*. https://climate.nasa.gov/effects

Robichaud, P. (2016). Is ignorance of climate change culpable? *Science and Engineering Ethics, 23,* 1409–1430. https://doi.org/10.1007/s11948-016-9835-5

Thomson, J. J. (1971). A defense of abortion. *Philosophy and Public Affairs, 1*(1), 47–66. https:// www.jstor.org/stable/2265091

United States Environmental Protection Agency. (2019). *Sources of greenhouse gas emissions*. https://www.epa.gov/ghgemissions/sources-greenhouse-gas-emissions

PART IV
SEX

Chapter 13

What Is Gender?

by
Celeste Johnson

[Alan and Dana are having lunch in the cafeteria at school.]

Alan: Look, Dana! There's the new kid. I can't tell if it's a girl who looks like a guy or a guy who looks like a girl.

Dana: That's Jesse. They're nonbinary.

Alan: What's that supposed to mean?

Dana: It means Jesse doesn't consider themselves either gender.

Alan: But how is that possible? Either you have female genitals or male genitals.

Dana: First of all, some people are born with both or neither genitals. Secondly, having, say, female genitals doesn't mean you have to identify with the feminine gender. Jesse prefers not to be called by the pronouns "she" or "her."

Alan: But doesn't that mean that Jesse is really a girl?

Dana: When you say "really" you assume that gender is an essential quality that people are born with. But if you think about it, all of the factors that constitute gender—like wearing makeup and dresses, liking pink and baby dolls, and excelling in service roles—are behaviors we learn after birth.

Alan: I thought girls naturally prefer feminine things.

DOI: 10.4324/9781003238393-18

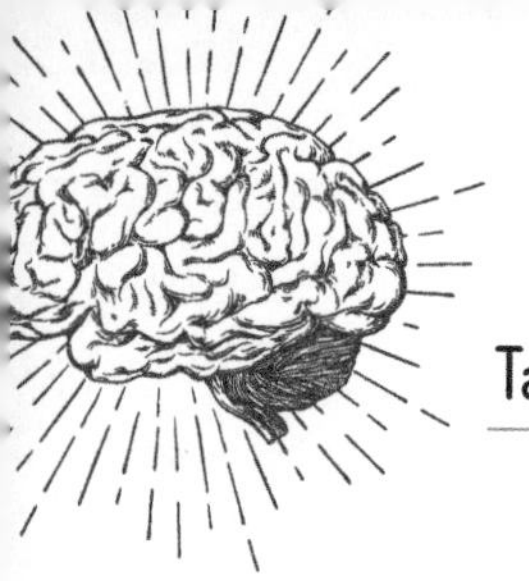

Dana: Really? How do you know? Suppose you were born on a different planet where babies with penises were raised with feminine things, while babies with vaginas were raised with masculine things.

Alan: Hmmm . . . I just don't think you can separate sex and gender like that. What if the babies with penises start shooting their dolls at each other, while the babies with vaginas start cuddling their trucks and rocking them to sleep?

Dana: Maybe it would be easier for you to imagine a planet where there is no gender. There, people have penises or vaginas, but you don't know which unless you see them naked because people all wear unisex clothes and haircuts. They also use unisex pronouns and have unisex bathrooms.

Alan: Why would you want to hide the truth about your genitals like that? You should outwardly display what you are and let people refer to you accordingly.

Dana: But why? Think about it. It would be impossible to discriminate against women if you didn't know which people had vaginas and which had penises. When you call someone "she" or "her," you're putting them in a limited category that has been discriminated against for all of history.

Alan: Well, I'm happy with my sex and my gender. But if Jesse isn't, then I guess can respect them and their pronouns.

Intersex: A term used to describe people whose genitals do not conform to the typical male or female model.

Transgender: A term used to describe people who have chosen a gender that does not correspond with their birth sex.

According to Merriam-Webster, gender is "the behavioral, cultural, or psychological traits typically associated with one sex." Notice that this definition posits only a *typical association* between sex and gender. Yet throughout Western history, the terms *sex* and *gender* have often been used interchangeably. For example, when you complete a form concerning your personal information, it may ask for your sex or your gender, as though these terms were synonyms. Furthermore, the form may give you a choice to circle "M" or "F." The assumption that sex and gender are the same and that they are binary—just two possibilities—is being challenged more than ever before in popular culture today.

An umbrella term for individuals who do not conform to long-held Western beliefs about masculinity and femininity is *gender-nonconforming*, or GNC. Jesse is a gender-nonconforming individual who provides an example of the distinction between sex and gender. Although Dana and Jesse may have the same genitals, they prefer different pronouns: Dana goes by the feminine pronouns *she* and *her*, while Jesse goes by the neutral pronouns *they* and *them*. Dana tries to convince Alan that Jesse is entitled to choose a gender identity regardless of biological sex.

What do you think of Dana's argument? Philosophers have debated both sides of the issue. One side can be called *gender essentialism*. The other side can be called *gender constructionism*.

Gender essentialism can be defined as the view that the psychological and physical traits of men and women are inherent and unchanging and that "male" and "female" are

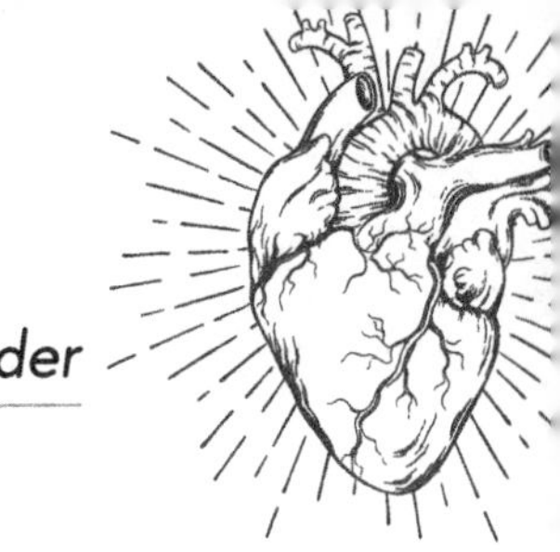

the only two genders that exist. This view has been so dominant throughout history that very few philosophers have taken the time to defend it. It is simply assumed to be true. Nevertheless, philosophers use the assumption that there are innately masculine and feminine traits to justify sexist attitudes. For example, the ancient Greek philosopher Aristotle wrote that "the male . . . is by nature more expert at leading than the female." Likewise, 19th-century philosopher Arthur Schopenhauer wrote, "One need only look at a woman's shape to discover that she is not intended for either too much mental or too much physical work." For both Aristotle and Schopenhauer, women were inferior to men due to the differences in their bodies.

Although overt sexism like this is diminishing, many people still believe masculine and feminine behaviors are naturally tied to birth sex. The growing knowledge of human physiology can provide support for this view. It has long been known that men are, on average, taller, heavier, stronger, and quicker than women. Anyone who watches the Olympics knows that it would not be fair to pit men against women in any but a few sports.

Now that women are allowed to have the same education as men, it has become clear that there is no innate difference in intelligence between the sexes. Nevertheless, there are measurable differences in the brains of men and women. For example, neurologist Joe Herbert wrote that an area of the hypothalamus, part of the brain known to be concerned with sexuality (but also with eating, drinking, aggression and other means of survival), is larger in males than females, and smaller in male-to-female transgender brains. Although he granted that scientists don't yet know what this size difference means, he used it to support his conclusion that gender identity is determined in the brain.

Gender essentialists reason as follows: At the time of conception, most human beings either receive two X chromosomes or an X and a Y chromosome. The former usually develop a vagina along with a host of other female sex traits, while the later usually develop a penis along with a host of other male sex traits. Among these sex traits are chemicals (such as hormones) and structures (such as neural assemblies) that cause gender disposi-

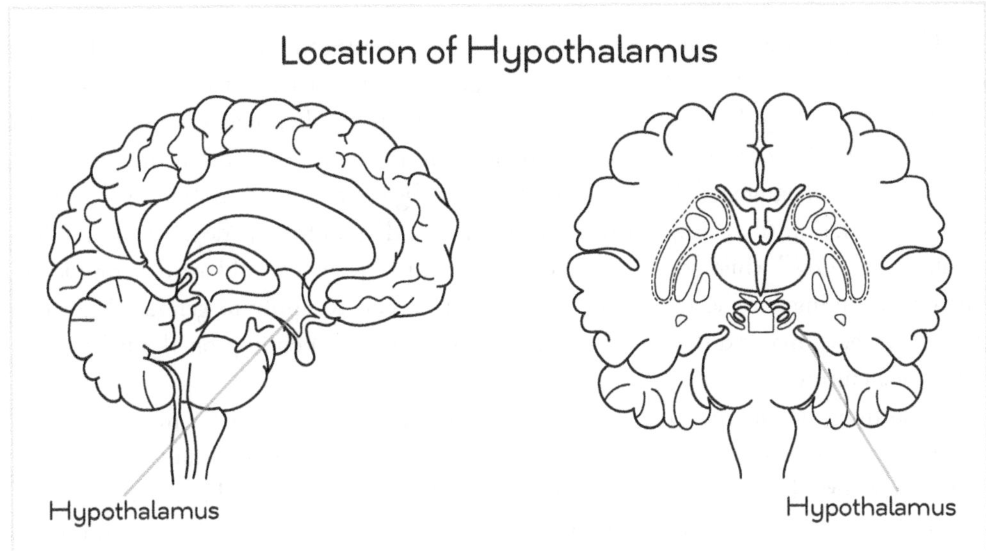

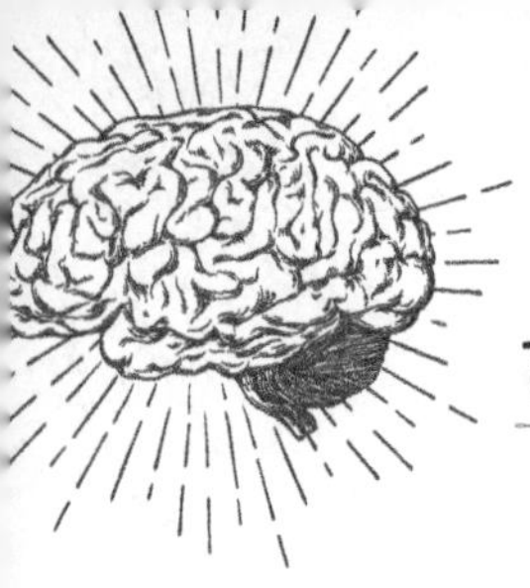

Determinism: The thesis that there is no such thing as free will; genes and past experiences determine who people will become.

Indeterminism: The thesis that human beings have free will that enables them to choose who they will become.

tions. For example, boys will typically be born with a disposition for rough play, while girls will typically be born with a disposition for gentle play.

Gender essentialists will grant that, although specific gender behaviors are imposed by culture, the underlying dispositions are innate. For example, although there is nothing natural about makeup and nail polish, there is something very natural about females wanting to decorate their bodies to attract a mate. Gender essentialists may consider intersex individuals to be rare exceptions based on chromosomal anomalies. Likewise, they may consider someone who does not identify with their gender as suffering from dysphasia, a psychological disorder that could be treated once its causes are better understood.

The Gender Essentialist Argument

1. Sex traits (chromosomes, genitals, etc.) are innate.
2. Gender behavior is caused by sex traits.
3. Therefore, gender behavior is innate.

Critics of gender essentialism point out that this viewpoint presupposes that human personalities are physically determined. This is a controversial thesis. Many people believe that, even if genetic makeup influences behavior, people still have the freedom to go along with those influences or go against them. According to this indetermininist view, someone might choose not to behave in a feminine way even if they have female sex traits. Having this control might be empowering for many individuals.

Critics are further concerned about the idea of treating dissatisfaction with one's gender as a disorder. When homosexuality was treated as a disorder in the 20th century, it led to cruel experiments and treatments. Why should the scientific community be allowed to impose a rigid binary gender system onto society? The transgender movement sees gender fluidity as a healthy alternative that could help to end sexual discrimination once and for all.

Gender constructionism is an alternative to the idea that there are inherent biological traits for males and females. It holds that gender is a social construct, manufactured arbitrarily by society. If society were to collapse tomorrow, then gender would have no real meaning. Many aspects of human experience in the world have been constructed by society, including language. For instance, the word *dog* is a meaningless sound for a native Spanish speaker until an English speaker points to a dog and says, "dog." If the English speaker said, "dog," while pointing to a cat, the Spanish speaker would learn a completely different meaning for the word. The same could be said to apply to gender. The word *female* can have many different meanings across cultures depending on the beliefs and values of a culture.

According to constructionists, society constructed the female gender in order to discriminate against women. The French feminist philosopher Simon de Beauvoir wrote that "one is not born, but rather becomes a woman." Although she granted that there are biological differences between men and women, she contended that there is no justification

for viewing women as inferior. She showed how women are not innately feminine but rather conditioned to behave in feminine ways. Recall that Aristotle and Schopenhauer regarded women as less fit than men for leading or doing mental or physical work. De Beauvoir maintained that, if this is true, it is only because of the social circumstances women have been subjected to. For example, it is difficult to shovel snow in high heels.

American philosopher Judith Butler argued that gender is much like a theatrical performance in which the players put on costumes, speak their lines, and play their part. In her view, someone with a vagina could just as easily play the part of a man, and someone with a penis could just as easily play the part of a woman. For Butler, gender "is real only to the extent that it is performed." The sooner people realize that they are playing roles written for them by society, the sooner they can break out of these roles and find freedom.

Although de Beauvoir saw gender as a social construct, Butler went further in seeing both gender and sex as social constructions, because neither could exist outside of the words people use for them. For example, there are no special words for "big ears" versus "little ears." If people had no special words for "penis" versus "vagina," they would be unable to distinguish between biological males and females. Butler envisioned a world that doesn't make such a big deal out of reproductive functions.

Judith Butler

Finally, some scientific research has shown that biological differences may not be as real as people think they are. Neuroscientist Gina Rippon wrote that significant differences between male and female brains do not actually exist and have been overemphasized by sexist science. Like de Beauvoir and Butler, Rippon believed that "a gendered world will produce a gendered brain," and she supported this claim using neuroscientific research that demonstrates how neurological pathways in the brain are shaped by social influence.

Gender constructionism directly challenges sexual discrimination but presents some significant questions. The reason human beings make such a big deal out of reproductive function is because reproducing has been crucial to the survival of the species for millennia. Even today, mating to form a family is a central part of many human lives. Male and female genders are the key markers for designating reproductive potential.

Still, should those who are uninterested in reproduction be forced to live by concepts designed to support successful mating? Just how flexible is human culture, and how much innovation can language accommodate?

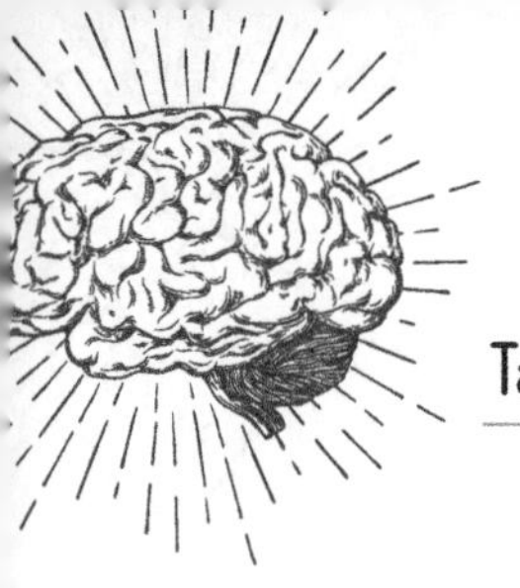

Personal Statement

As a nonbinary trans person, I constantly struggle with presenting myself in a way that is taken seriously and respected by other people but is also true to how I personally view my body and my identity. I do not regard myself as male or female, and I ask others to do the same because I truly believe that I am neither male nor female. To exist outside of such a longstanding gender binary brings new challenges every day, and I often find myself frustrated with how society has viewed gender. But regardless of whether you believe in gender or not, it is important to continue having discussions about what it means to have a gender or to be a certain sex.

Discussion Questions

1. Have you ever come across any instances of gender nonconformity?
2. What are some issues today that arise due to people being treated differently based on gender?
3. Why do you think society has generally viewed gender as objective and unchanging?
4. Do you agree more with gender essentialism or constructionism? In what ways?
5. What other examples of social construction (besides gender) can you think of?

Classroom Activities

1. Put on a play (or read a script) in which the females play male characters and the males play female characters. Discuss how it felt to play the opposite gender and how it affected the play.
2. Watch and discuss a TED Talk about an intersex or transgender individual.

References

Aristotle. (1895). *Aristotle's politics: A treatise on government* (W. Ellis, Trans.). Routledge and Sons. (Original work published ca. 350 BCE)

Butler, J. (1988). Performative acts and gender constitution: An essay in phenomenology and feminist theory. *Theatre Journal, 40*(4), 519–531. https://doi.org/10.2307/3207893

de Beauvoir, S. (2011). *The second sex* (C. Borde & S. Malovany-Chevallier, Trans.). Knopf Doubleday. (Original work published 1949)

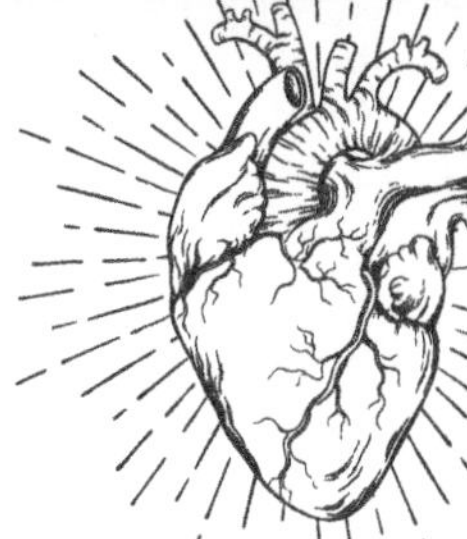

Herbert, J. (2016). *Gender identity is in the brain. What does this tell us?* Psychology Today. https://www.psychologytoday.com/us/blog/hormones-and-the-brain/201608/gender-identity-is-in-the-brain-what-does-tell-us

Rippon, G. (2019). *The gendered brain: The new neuroscience that shatters the myth of the female brain.* Vintage.

Schopenhauer, A. (2016). *Studies in pessimism: A series of essays* (T. B. Saunders, Trans.). Dancing Unicorn Books. (Original work published 1893).

Chapter 14

Is Monogamy Necessary?

by
Autumn Franz

[Taylor and Justice are shopping together for something fun to wear to a party at Sam's house this weekend.]

Taylor: You know, I really do love Sam, but . . . can I tell you a secret? Lately, I've found myself strongly attracted to Alex, too. I really want to be with both of them, and I don't think I can choose.

Justice: Well, you have to choose.

Taylor: But maybe I don't.

Justice: What? You can't love more than one person at the same time.

Taylor: Why not? I have more than one best friend—you, Imanee, and Jordan—and I love all of you. Why can't I do the same with multiple romantic partners?

Justice: Because there's an important difference between love for a friend and love for a romantic partner—namely, physical intimacy. You can't have more than one lover.

Taylor: Who says? Our society created that expectation back when people got married and started families at the age of 15. Romantic love doesn't have to be about producing a family anymore.

DOI: 10.4324/9781003238393-19

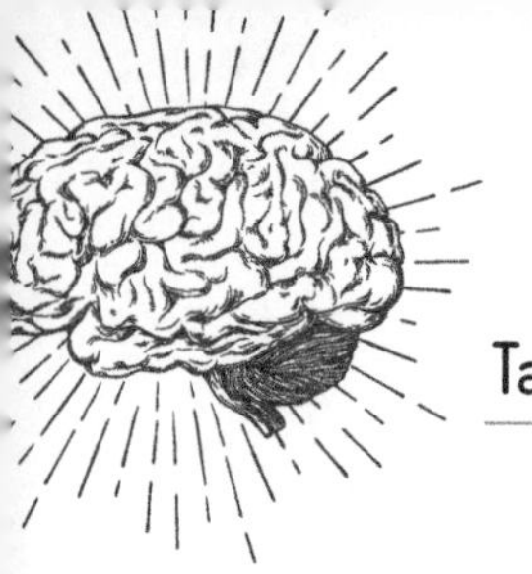

Justice: Well, I think our biology still predisposes us to be with only one person. I would feel so betrayed and jealous if Shay wasn't satisfied with just me. And I'm not alone in this. I mean, otherwise, why haven't more people had more than one lover at the same time?

Monogamy, from the Greek words for "one" and "marriage," means having one romantic partner one's whole life.

Taylor: They have! It's just that society shames everyone into being secretive about it. Why sneak around? If I have feelings for more than one person, it must be natural. Why should I feel bad and try to resist it?

Justice: Because you can hurt people, Taylor. If you suggest to Sam and Alex that you want to date both of them, they might think that you're selfish and don't actually care about either of them. How would you feel if Sam wanted to date someone else while still dating you?

Taylor: I'd be totally cool with that.

Justice: Really?

Taylor: Yeah, I think it's only fair that Sam could be with other people because I would be, too.

Love is a phenomenon that philosophers have grappled with since ancient Greece. Today love plagues the minds of musicians, poets, and philosophers alike. People read about love in teen novels, watch rom-coms, and spend thousands of dollars on weddings and Valentine's Day gifts. Love is a major focus of human life, but not just any type of love: romantic love.

People often use words like *dedicated* or *committed* to talk about romantic love because couples are traditionally monogamous. Although monogamy is common practice, it is not the only way of conducting a romantic relationship. Polyamory, also known as consensual nonmonogamy, refers to the practice of openly having more than one lover at the same time.

In a society dominated by monogamy, polyamory is dismissed as a fancy word for cheating. There is no question that the practice of having more than one lover has been common throughout history. And there is no question that this practice is sometimes harmful. If a person promises their lover that they will commit to them alone, and then sneaks around with someone else, then they have broken a promise, which is hurtful. But what about cases in which romantic partners agree to allow each other to have additional partners? Is this is possible? Or is monogamy necessary for human beings?

Biologist Matt Ridley argued that monogamy is necessary. He defended the practice of committing to a single romantic partner as both natural and beneficial to the human species. In his view, monogamy arose through the process of evolution. Evolution designed human beings for one purpose only, sex, because sex is the only way humans can pass on genes to the next generation. Genes are the building blocks of human beings. Because they want to survive for as long as possible, humans have a natural urge to reproduce and spread their genes to the next generation. Each person is the descendent of successful reproducers and has inherited the genes of those who have won the reproduction game.

But this game plays out differently for males and females. Each sex uses romantic partnership to accomplish a different goal. For males, romantic partnership is mostly the promise of an orgasm, which gives males motivation to seek out sexual encounters as often as possible. For females, romantic partnership is mostly the promise of help with raising the offspring. For a female, heterosexual activity could result in pregnancy, which will monopolize at least a year of her time and energy. Although she can do it alone, resources provided by the father will make it more likely for the offspring to survive. Therefore, she has great incentive to make him commit to her, instead of spending his time and energy on other mates.

Why would a male ever agree to such a commitment? Ridley explained the cleverness of the male strategy. Assume that every male is competing with every other male to mate with as many females as possible. Because some males are naturally stronger, faster, smarter, or more seductive than the others, they will tend to impregnate a larger than average percentage of the female population. With most of the females pregnant for many months, most of the males will have no chance at reproducing at all. If they do nothing about this, their genes will not make it to the next generation—game over. So they make a tradeoff with the females. In exchange for the opportunity to mate, they will help with childrearing. Ridley contended that this reproductive strategy has been extremely successful. It explains why most men agree to be monogamous.

Still, both men and women have been known to cheat; cheating is part of the evolutionary game for both sexes. The purpose of monogamy is to partner two individuals for greater success in reproduction. But there are still individuals outside the relationship who carry better genes. In fact, said Ridley, the males who are stronger, faster, smarter, or more seductive never bothered to partner up because they knew they were already winning the game. A male will always be tempted to try to behave like one of the lucky few who doesn't need to partner up. A brief fling will enable him to spread his genes, leaving them to be raised by some other male. Meanwhile, females who sneak off with the superior males will become impregnated with better genes while leaving their less competitive husbands to raise the offspring.

All of this behavior, Ridley claimed, is perfectly natural. Although it may look like polyamory at first glance, closer analysis proves otherwise. From a biological point of view, both men and women marry to trick their partner into giving them what they desire. A man must pretend to be wholly enamored with a woman to gain access to consistent sex, while occasionally searching for another option in secret. Meanwhile, a woman must pretend to be faithful to her second-rate husband, while looking for the opportunity to produce children with first-rate seducers behind his back.

From Ridley's perspective, human beings have been playing the monogamy game for millions of years. If this is truly the case, then it is no wonder that people become irrationally angry about cheaters. In the age of birth control, people don't have to play the monogamy game anymore, at least not for reproduction's sake. Having sex with someone other than one's romantic partner need not have reproductive implications. People's minds know this, but their bodies don't. Raising someone else's child is a complete waste of one's life, from the point of view of genes. No wonder, then, that people are likely to feel jeal-

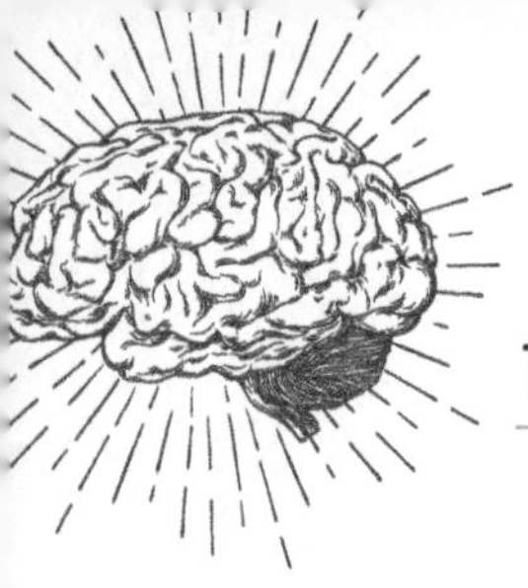

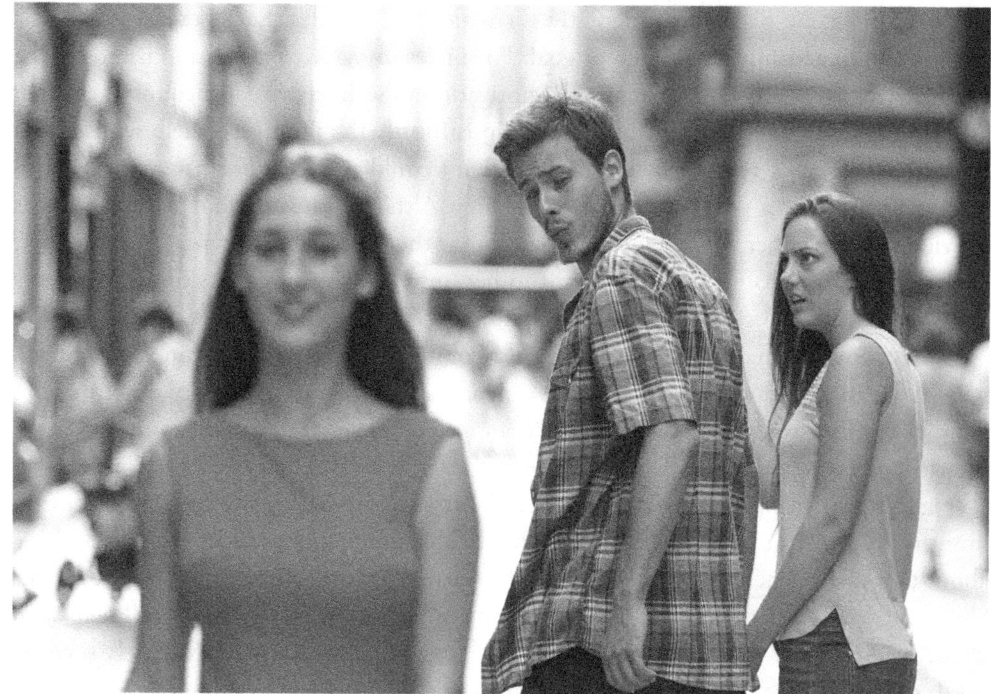

ous, betrayed, and even homicidal the moment their romantic partner gives the hint of an interest in someone else.

From Ridley's point of view, traditional monogamy has always involved secret cheating. If the extramarital affairs were to happen in the open, the couple would simply be called polyamorous. But extramarital affairs don't happen in the open, and there is good reason: Secret cheating provides an evolutionary benefit, for the reasons mentioned previously. Ridley deemed anything that provides an evolutionary benefit to be natural—and anything that is natural is necessary. He did not exactly condemn polyamory as immoral. But he did condemn it as unnatural and ultimately harmful to humanity.

Ridley's Argument **FOR** Monogamy

1. Natural selection programs human beings to prefer monogamy.
2. Whatever natural selection programs human beings to prefer is necessary.
3. Therefore, monogamy is necessary.

Philosopher Carrie Jenkins disagreed. Although granting that romantic love is partly determined by biology, she insisted that it is also partly determined by social norms. She used an analogy to make her case. Consider an actor named Jaylen playing a character named Hans in a theater performance. While watching, you may notice some features that belong to Jaylen and others that belong to Hans. For instance, Jaylen is Australian and normally speaks with an Australian accent, while his character Hans is German and speaks

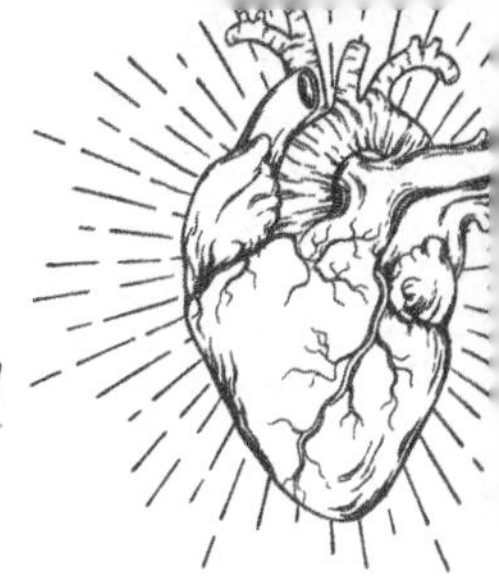

with a German accent. Although one feature may belong to Hans and another to Jaylen, the person you see in the performance is a combination of actor and character, not one or the other. Jenkins stated, "Romantic love is like this. Some of our ancient, evolved biological machinery—a collection of neural pathways and chemical responses—is currently playing the starring role of Romantic Love in a show called *Modern Society*."

Social norm: An unwritten rule that members of society are expected to obey.

Jenkins argued that biology and social norms both determine how romantic love works. According to this analogy, biology is the actor, and social norms are the character. The difficulty lies in determining which is which. The biological aspect of romantic love is not something people create but instead discover within themselves. Because humans cannot change their biology, whatever it contributes to romantic love is necessary. However, social norms contribute a lot as well, and people can change these as well as create them anew, although this does not mean they can pick and choose whichever social norms they like and leave the rest behind. Social norms also affect the way people understand romantic love in modern society. Although norms may define what romantic love is now, these aspects of romantic love have not always been present, and they will not always be. Both biology and social norms are crucial because leaving one of the two behind will prevent truly understanding what romantic love is.

Is monogamy biologically necessary, or is it just a social norm? Although Ridley pointed to reproduction and childrearing to prove it is biologically necessary, others have challenged this assumption. Jenkins argued that monogamy is a complicated way to make childrearing easier. There are much simpler solutions. For example, say the problem that mothers were having was the need to do work while watching their baby at the same time. In this instance, creating a baby sling out of cloth would be a snap compared to convincing all fathers to watch the children. It would be much harder for evolution to produce monogamy than a baby sling.

Furthermore, Ridley implied that the male sex drive makes males reluctant partners in monogamy. But Jenkins pointed to research indicating that women are just as likely as men to grow tired of monogamy. A study done by psychologist Dietrich Klusmann found that heterosexual women are actually more likely to lose sexual desire for their partner in a long-term monogamous relationship than men are. Although both men and women in the study were found to have equal lust for their partners in the beginning of their relationships, sexual motivation declined in women but not in men. Jenkins warned against being too quick to explain romantic love on the basis of primitive biological processes.

But even supposing that monogamy is mostly determined by a social norm, is it really changeable? Jenkins granted that a social norm may be very difficult to change. She acknowledged that she cannot escape the fact that society views her polyamorous relationship as cheating. Although she could try to stop caring how society views her, she cannot force others to stop caring about those norms.

Still, there is reason for hope. For example, racist individuals used to think Africans were naturally suited to slavery. Likewise, sexist individuals used to think women were naturally incapable of voting. Over time, with the help of brave activists, people realized that these social norms needed to change. Even ideals of love have changed. The U.S. has eradicated laws against interracial marriage and gay marriage, changing oppressive social

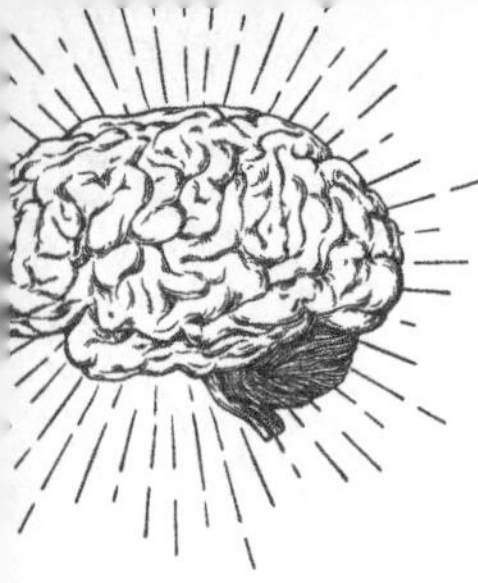

norms. Jenkins hoped society might likewise begin to reevaluate monogamy. If it is mostly a social norm, then it is not necessary, and people do have the power to change its perception, even if it takes a long time.

Jenkins's Argument *AGAINST* Monogamy

1. Monogamy is at least partly a social norm.
2. Any social norm can be changed.
3. Anything that can be changed is not necessary.
4. Therefore, monogamy is not completely necessary.

Personal Statement

I have spent a lot of time considering the question this chapter asks because I myself have been in multiple romantic relationships at the same time. In my experience of polyamory, all three of my partners were at the same level. By "same level," I mean that although I loved each of them uniquely, I also gave them equal priority and attention. What I valued most about these relationships was that I was able to move away from social standards of possessiveness and hiding of true emotions and move toward radical honesty and a rejection of jealousy.

Although I have experienced the feeling of loving more than one person at the same time, like Jenkins, I wonder if it is really possible to do in the world today without hurting people. I want to deny Ridley's claim that I am confined to acting a certain way based on my gender, but I also know that how people perceive my gender is important to me.

I'd like to think love isn't determined only by biology and social norms. In a very Platonic way, I believe love could exist outside of what people perceive it to be. What I mean by this is that love is beyond human understanding. People recognize a shadow of it in the world and try to live it according to this limited perspective. When they do this, they focus on what society believes instead of trying to find the objective truth about love. And when people moved away from the true focus—love itself, or knowledge itself, or beauty itself—then they have no way to truly achieve it. Maybe people are too focused on what the world thinks, instead of what is beautiful, good, and true.

Discussion Questions

1. In your view, is romantic love determined by biology, social norms, both, or something else? Explain.
2. Is love an evolutionary tool or something more? If love is an evolutionary tool, does that mean it's not *real*?
3. Compare and contrast polyamory and monogamy. What are some features of polyamory that you like? What are some features of monogamy that you like?
4. What is important to you in a relationship? Do any of these values overlap with features of polyamory or monogamy? Which ones?
5. Most people have a negative view of polyamory. When thinking of the negative characteristics of polyamory, are these characteristics exclusive to polyamory? Or does monogamy have the possibility of carrying these characteristics as well?

Classroom Activities

1. Interview family and friends concerning their experiences with monogamy, polyandry, and cheating. Discuss your most interesting findings. (Use pseudonyms to protect the privacy of your interviewees.)
2. Write and share essays arguing that polyandry is or is not immoral.

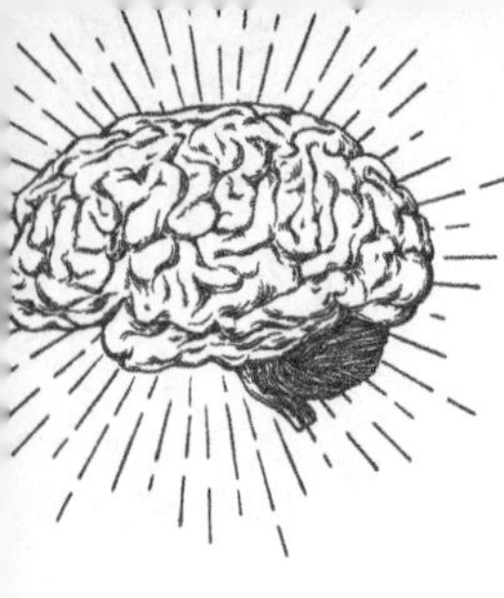

References

Jenkins, C. (2017). *What love is and what it could be.* Basic Books.

Ridley, M. (2003). *The red queen: Sex and the evolution of human nature.* Harper Perennial. (Original work published 1993)

Chapter 15

Is Pornography Immoral?

by
Celeste Johnson

[Liz sees Maggie reading at the library and sits down next to her.]

Liz: Hey, Maggie, can I talk to you about something? It's about Troy. Things have been going well with him, but I found out the other night that he watches porn. A lot of it.

Maggie: A lot of boys watch porn. What's the big deal?

Liz: Well, have you watched any? It's so degrading to women—the way most of them have the same stereotypical look and the way the men treat them. So much of it is clearly made for straight men—even the lesbian porn! I feel like it gives everyone the wrong idea about what sex should be and encourages men to mistreat women.

Maggie: I mean, yeah, a lot of porn is like you say it is, but not all of it. Some porn really is made for queer people and feminist-minded people as well. Heck, there's even a Feminist Porn Award. Some of the women in porn really like their jobs, and even if it looks like they're being treated badly, it's all carefully staged on a film set. They are actually pretty safe.

Liz: I'm sure some of the women like their jobs, and they may be safe most of the time, but that doesn't change the fact that it *looks* like they're treated badly. I don't know. I just think it gives boys the wrong idea, and I'm worried Troy will take it at face value, and I'll have to deal with it down the road.

DOI: 10.4324/9781003238393-20

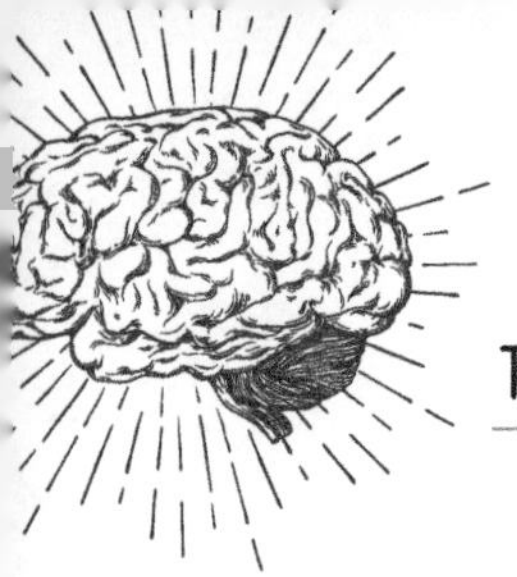

Maggie: Yeah, I understand what you're saying. It might be worth trying to talk some of this out with him. Maybe if he knows some of the concerns, he'll be less likely to absorb the bad messaging.

First-wave feminism: This wave took place in the 19th and early 20th century. First-wave feminists supported the Temperance Movement, the abolition of slavery, and women's suffrage (the right to vote).

Second-wave feminism: This wave took place from the 1960s to the 1980s. Second-wave feminists were concerned with women's relegation to the home. The phrase "the personal is political" became a lasting feminist insight into oppression. During this wave, many traditionally feminine qualities were critiqued and rejected, and sexual objectification came under scrutiny.

Illustration by Seth Troyer

Although sex education is part of the health curriculum at many schools, these classes are not likely to address the sexual can of worms that is pornography. Pornography is, simply put, the representation of sex and sexual activity in a visual format—printed, filmed, or otherwise. Although it may seem that pornography needs no special consideration in sex education, this is not the case. The content of pornography, and how it is consumed both by individuals and by society at large, raises many important ethical questions. To live a good life, whether or not it involves the consumption of pornography, one must evaluate the important moral and political conversations surrounding the topic.

One philosophical arena in which the ethics of pornography have been thoroughly explored is feminist philosophy. Although many second-wave feminists like Andrea Dworkin and Catharine MacKinnon strongly opposed contemporary pornography and its role in society, other feminists at the time, and many more third-wave feminists, offered a less black-and-white view. Some found some pornography to be problematic, but many found some pornography to be explicitly feminist. Third-wave feminists also, on the whole, were more likely to support a woman's right to choose a career in pornography. This split in feminist discourse produced an expansive back-and-forth debate on the topic.

Although there are many voices in this arena, this chapter will look at the contrasting perspectives of Andrea Dworkin and Nadine Strossen. These two philosophers can help better explain both Liz's and Maggie's perspectives on the issue.

Dworkin argued that "the major theme of pornography as a genre is men's power," a power which is affirmed in all aspects of life. Pornography reinforces many aspects of male power, including "the power of self, physical power over and against others, the power of terror, the power of naming, the power of owning, the power of money, and the power of sex." Dworkin argued that these aspects of male power are embedded in pornography—they are inseparable. If the first theme of pornography is asserting male dominance, then the secondary theme is the devaluation of women. According to Dworkin, women are degraded in pornography to "celebrate male power" and are valued less than men.

For Dworkin, pornography reinforces the reduction of women to purely sexual objects at the will of men. It also reinforces the notion that women do not have control over their own bodies. This undermines the possibility for men and women to have consensual sex. Objects cannot consent, and need not consent, to be used. If women are reduced to objects, then the same is true of them. This was, of course, troubling to Dworkin. Whether pornography is simply a reflection of the existing ideology of male supremacy or it is perpetuating this ideology, it is harmful for women.

Because of the message that women are sexual objects to be used by men, women do not truly have the free choice to perform in pornography. According to Dworkin, the woman who chooses to participate in commercialized sex is "being massively consumed,

Third-wave feminism: This wave began in the 1990s. Third-wave feminists set out to correct perceived failures of second-wave feminists, including the lack of inclusion of many important particulars like class, race, ability, and nonbinary gender identities. Third-wave feminists also rejected clear-cut, black-and-white answers for how women should act in a patriarchal society.

Illustration by Seth Troyer

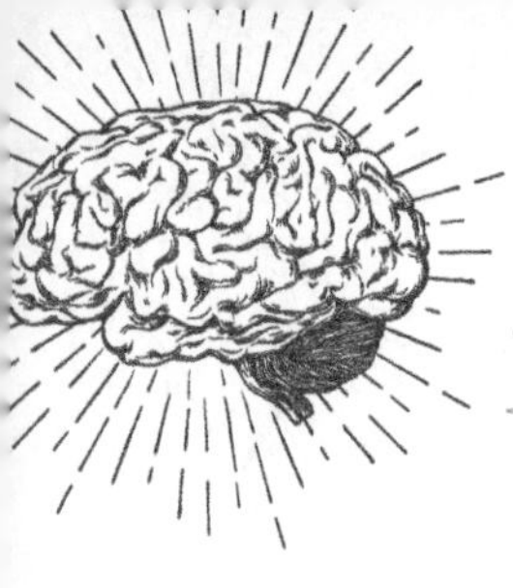

denied an individual nature, [and] denied any sexual sensibility other than that which serves the male." Men, who have power and control, are ultimately the ones profiting off of this "free" choice made by women entering the sex industry. Male power undermines the ability for women to make a free choice in this arena.

Dworkin's Argument *AGAINST* Pornography

1. Pornography makes women into objects.
2. Making a person into an object is immoral.
3. Therefore, pornography is immoral.

Although Strossen shared Dworkin's fear, anger, and frustration with male supremacy and gender-based violence, she did not believe that censoring or eliminating pornography is the solution to the problem. In fact, she argued that censoring pornography would do more harm than good for the situation of women. Strossen argued that "women should not have to choose between freedom and safety." Restricting women's choices around sexuality also compromises their freedom for the sake of their safety, which should not be the case.

Strossen claimed that women are much more threatened by legal restriction of their rights than by the existence of pornography. The restriction of rights, even "for their own

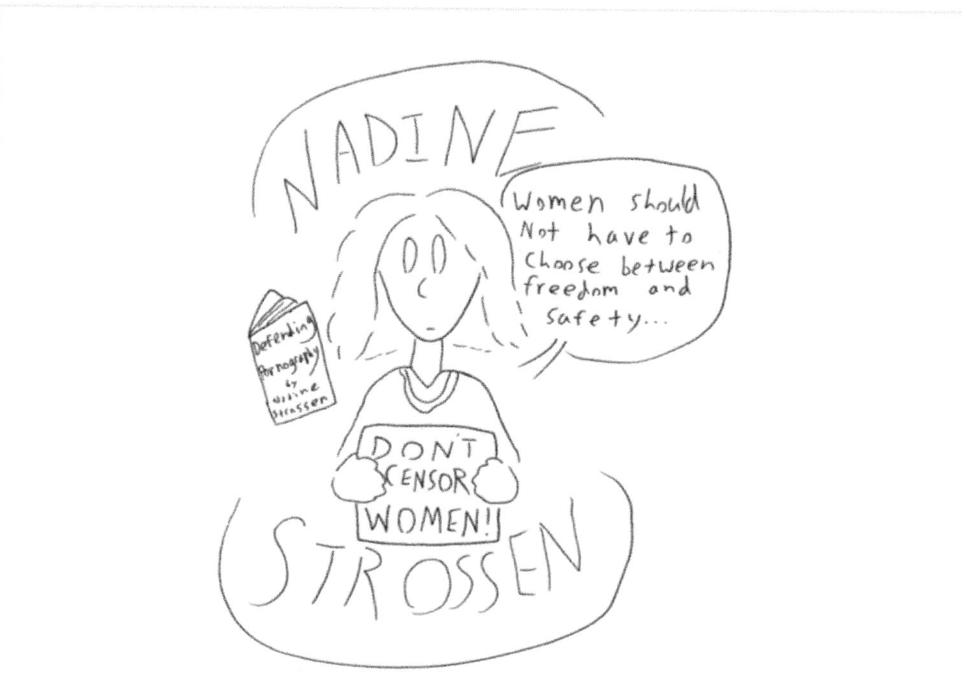

Illustration by Seth Troyer

good," erodes autonomy, the freedom crucial to being a person. Strossen worried about how restrictions on pornography would actually play out, noting that "all censorship measures throughout history have been used disproportionately to silence those who are relatively dis-empowered and who seek to challenge the status quo." Because women and feminists are of that category, she worried that the government may target those it allegedly seeks to protect through these restrictions. Pornography is a form of sexual expression that should be available and accessible to women as an outlet for their sexuality.

Strossen also disagreed with Dworkin that all pornographic material is exploitative of women. Women, if allowed the freedom to express themselves sexually as they please, are better able to undermine misogyny. She cited lesbian pornography, specifically, as being an area of positive sexual expression for women. This kind of porn can subvert harmful sexual expectations. She also noted that sexually explicit materials can be made by women portraying feminist values, again subverting masculine expectations.

Strossen's Argument *FOR* Pornography

1. Pornography is a form of freedom of expression.
2. Exercising one's freedom of expression is not immoral.
3. Therefore, pornography is not immoral.

Personal Statement

Revisiting the dialogue from the start of this chapter, it seems that Liz's perspective is mostly supported by Dworkin's work, while Maggie's perspective is mostly supported by Strossen's. Although Liz's and Maggie's perspectives may differ, they are both speaking from a place of concern for the well-being of those who work in the porn industry as well as women as a whole. This is also the case between Dworkin and Strossen. The two disagree, however, on the best way to improve the situation of women broadly.

Whether to consume pornography or not is a personal choice—a choice ideally made with consideration, care, and caution. Those who do choose to watch porn, however, may want to consider Maggie's last remark to Liz. Perhaps simply being aware of the dialogue around the ethics of pornography will prove beneficial for even the casual porn consumer.

Discussion Questions

1. Have concerns about the safety or well-being of the actors in pornography come up at any time for you or a friend?
2. Do you feel comfortable openly discussing your thoughts, questions, and concerns about pornography?
3. Have you learned about pornography in a classroom setting (like a sex education class)? Do you think this should be a topic discussed at school?

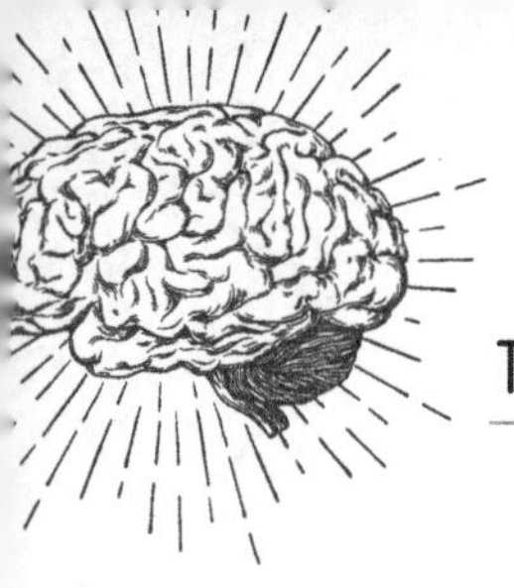

Discussion Questions, *continued*

4. Do you agree more with Liz, who defends Dworkin's view, or Maggie, who defends Strossen's view? In what ways?
5. What critiques might you offer Dworkin or Strossen?

Classroom Activities

1. Hold a talk show about pornography. Everyone picks a character to play: talk show host, porn star, porn filmmaker, pornography user, girlfriend of pornography user, pornographic magazine producer, sexter, priest, etc. Perform nuanced perspectives for these characters.
2. Hold a debate on whether or not pornography is immoral.

References

Dworkin, A. (1981). *Pornography: Men possessing women.* Perigee Books.

Strossen, N. (1995). *Defending pornography: Free speech, sex, and the fight for women's rights.* Scribner.

Chapter 16

When Is a Person Ready to Have Sex?

by
Tommy Kegler

[Rick and Tara are watching a movie together in Rick's basement.]

Rick: Hey, Tara—you want to turn the movie off?

Tara: What do you mean?

Rick: I mean we should have sex! Everyone is asleep, and we're all alone. It's the perfect time.

Tara: I don't know Rick, I don't think we're ready. I was planning on waiting for a stronger connection . . . a permanent connection.

Rick: Aww, come on. We've been dating for 5 months now. Am I not special?

Tara: Of course you are. But this is an important decision, and I don't want to rush into it. Not to mention, I always wanted to give my first time to my husband.

Rick: So, you don't want me?

Tara: I'm not saying I want to break up! I just don't feel comfortable doing it before we commit to each other for life.

Rick: You're overthinking this. Sex is no big deal. Everyone is doing it anyway.

Tara: I don't care what other people are doing. Everyone has to make their own choices for their own reasons. I don't want to have sex right now because

DOI: 10.4324/9781003238393-21

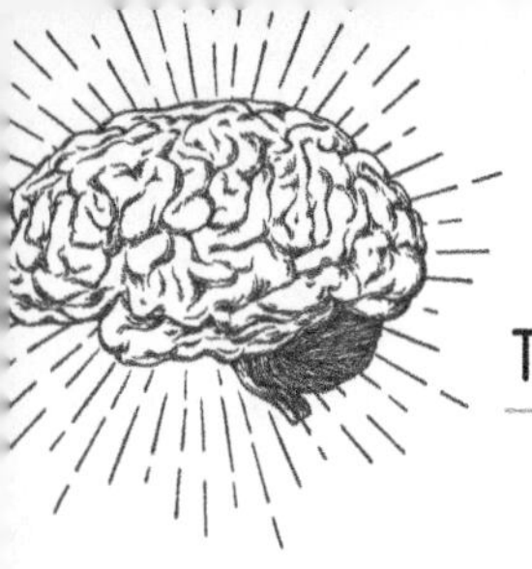

> I think sex is a big deal and should only be shared between committed people. Plus, what if one of us gets an STD or something?
>
> **Rick:** Are you saying you have something contagious?
>
> **Tara:** No.
>
> **Rick:** Well, neither do I. Plus, I have a condom, so we will be safe . . . I really want you, Tara. I've already proven my commitment to you by being with you all this time.
>
> **Tara:** Well, you can prove it even more by respecting my wishes. Now watch the movie! A fight's about to start.

Sacred: Something special to God.

Sex is a touchy subject, especially for young people. Some teens feel totally lost in a world of physical and emotional encounters, unready to face the life-altering decisions sex presents. Others, however, feel able to make responsible choices about sex and believe they should have the freedom to do so. Because there is such a wide range of possible attitudes, each person must ask themselves: *At what point am I ready?* This chapter will examine two main points of view from different thinkers on the topic: those who regard marriage as a requirement for sex and those who do not.

Some proponents of waiting until marriage use religion to justify their view. Although different religions present different considerations, the general claim is that sex is a sacred act meant for two people who have proven their commitment to each other through marriage. Having sex outside of marriage, therefore, is a sin.

Why would someone regard the act of sex as sacred? No doubt because it is capable of producing offspring, a very serious matter. Reliable birth control has been available for less than a century, a blink of the eye on the timeline of civilization. Prior to that, any act of heterosexual sex was liable to produce a new and vulnerable human being, who would need parents in order to survive. Deciding to have heterosexual sex was therefore practically equivalent to deciding to become a parent. Because being a good parent means supporting one's child, it means forming a family unit—hence, getting married.

Today, birth control is cheap, reliable, and readily available for most people in the United States. Therefore, deciding to have sex is no longer equivalent to deciding to become a parent. Yet many religious people still maintain that premarital sex is wrong. In fact, they go so far as to argue *against* using birth control. According to this view, sex is meant only for the purpose of reproducing; people should never have sex just for pleasure.

This view was championed by Catholic philosopher Augustine of Hippo. Augustine's personal experience led him to condemn sex without marriage. Before he became religious, Augustine was an unprincipled man, renowned for gambling, fighting, and sexual promiscuity. In his famous autobiography *Confessions*, he looked back on his youth with regret:

> I cared for nothing but to love and be loved. But my love went beyond the affection of one mind for another, beyond the arc of the bright beam

> of friendship. Bodily desire, like a morass, and adolescent sex, welled up within me, exuding mists, which clouded over and obscured my heart, so that I could not distinguish the clear light of true love from the murk of lust. . . . In my tender youth they swept me away over the precipice of my body's appetites and plunged me in the whirlpool of sin.

Exploitation: When a person takes unfair advantage of someone else to get what they want.

In Augustine's view, the great beauty of love is the nonphysical connection between two minds. The physical desire involved in sex ruins love by reducing the relationship to a way of getting pleasure for oneself.

Augustine's Argument *AGAINST* Premarital Sex

1. Premarital sex is based on bodily desire.
2. Bodily desire turns love to lust.
3. Lust is sinful.
4. Therefore, premarital sex is sinful.

Augustine was probably right that a relationship changes when sex is introduced. But was he correct to suggest that sex will ruin friendship and destroy true love? Why is it so hard to stay friends or keep true love alive without marriage? Philosopher David Gilboa is a secular proponent of marriage who shed some light on this issue. He argued that having premarital sex, and even living in a society that embraces premarital sex, is exploitative.

Augustine of Hippo

Why would someone consider premarital sex exploitative? After all, Gilboa was not talking about rape, but about two consenting individuals. Imagine, for example, that in the dialogue Tara changes her mind and decides to have sex with Rick. What would be wrong with that? Gilboa identified two reasons why consent, even among good friends, is not enough.

First, premarital sex places an unfair burden on women. As

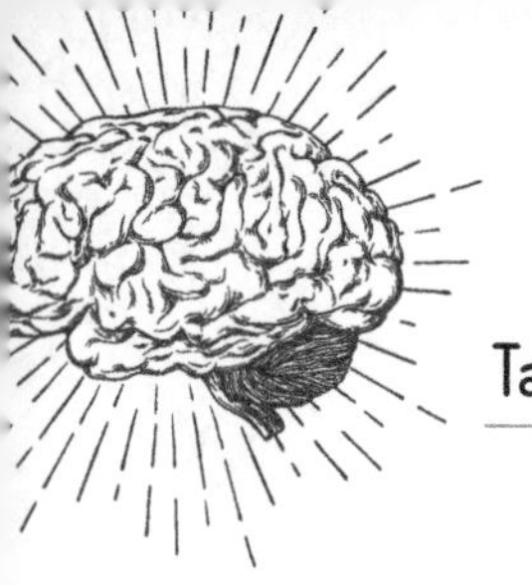

Feminism: The movement that seeks equal political, social, and economic rights for women. Different types of feminists define this equality differently.

Charles Darwin noted in his exhaustive study of evolution, the males of any species are generally more sexual than the females. Gilboa believed this is also the case with human beings: Men more often desire and initiate sex. So, the majority of the time, if a man and women are having sex, this will be because he wants to, not because she does. In other words, sex is typically a "favor" women are repeatedly asked to give. Of course, there is nothing wrong with giving favors. But there is something especially burdensome about the favor of sex: the high cost of pregnancy. Even if the chance is small, worry about that chance may be enough to take the fun out of the experience or even make the experience unpleasant. Marriage is the only way to force men to share that cost.

Second, premarital sex promotes peer pressure. Imagine you live in a world in which there is no such thing as marriage. All of your peers are having sex. You are in a relationship, but you are not ready for sex. Then one day your partner asks to have sex. You may feel that, if you refuse, your partner will leave you for someone else who can fulfill their sexual desires. So, living in a society where sex requires no commitment creates pressure. In the opposite society, where marriage is a prerequisite for sex, your partner could not leave you so easily, and so you would not feel that pressure.

Gilboa's Argument *AGAINST* Premarital Sex

1. Premarital sex puts burdens and pressures on women.
2. Putting burdens and pressures on people is wrong.
3. Therefore, premarital sex is wrong.

Although Augustine and Gilboa make some interesting points, there are those who disagree with their conclusion. The most compelling arguments in favor of premarital sex come from feminist theory. Feminists believe men and women should be able to partake in sexual activities on their own terms when they feel ready to do so. Even among feminists, however, opinions are split. Some maintain that sex is still a significant act that should be shared between two people who love each other or are special to one another. Others argue for casual sex, insisting that it can legitimately be shared by any two or more people who willingly consent, even if they have no emotional connection to one another.

Proponents of the significance view argue that people shouldn't have sex until they find a partner with whom they share a strong emotional connection. This partnership is needed for two reasons. First, partnerships help people to handle possible health issues. Even the strongest forms of birth control are not 100% effective. Because of this, every heterosexual experience has a chance of leading to pregnancy. Even if that chance is 1%, it is good for partners to have an understanding that they will support each other if the protection fails. Likewise, because casual sexual partners are not likely to know each other's sexual history, they are more likely to present a risk of spreading sexually transmitted diseases (STDs). Discussing sexual history with one's partner, getting tested, and building trust with one another can help to avoid this risk.

Second, partnerships ensure a positive sexual experience. Because different people have different tastes and expectations, it is good for sex partners to have a common understanding of each other in advance. If a person sets out to have sex with someone they meet at a party, they could easily be deceived into believing the encounter is safe when it is not. They may be lured into having sex that is unfulfilling or even traumatic. This problem could be avoided by having a strong connection with a partner before engaging in sex.

Of course, marriage is one way to form a strong emotional connection. Proponents of the significance view, however, insist that marriage is too restrictive, because it implies that a person should only have a single sexual partner for their whole life. According to the significance view, it may be healthier to have, or be open to having, a series of close partners. As people grow and develop, they may need new lovers, just as they need new friends, new careers, or new hobbies. According to the marriage view, breaking up is seen as a tragedy that damages the individuals. In contrast, according to the significance view, breaking up can be seen as a positive sign of growth.

The Argument *FOR* Significant Sex

1. Sex without a strong emotional connection subjects people to health risks, dissatisfaction, and trauma.
2. People should not subject others to health risks, dissatisfaction, and trauma.
3. Therefore, people should not have sex without a strong emotional connection.

Some feminists argue that good sex can be achieved without a strong emotional connection. After all, the chances of getting pregnant or contracting an STD are extremely low as long as couples are practicing safe sex. Ordering one's sexual life around the fear of these things can be crippling. Skiing is an extremely dangerous sport if skiers don't wear protective gear and don't know what they are doing. But this shouldn't keep responsible skiers from having fun.

Those who insist on a strong emotional connection seem to be concerned that casual partners will be likely to deceive others into having sex. But in that case, they should condemn deception, not casual sex. For example, suppose a sketchy company that constructed a bridge told you it was safe to cross, and then it collapsed when you were crossing it. The

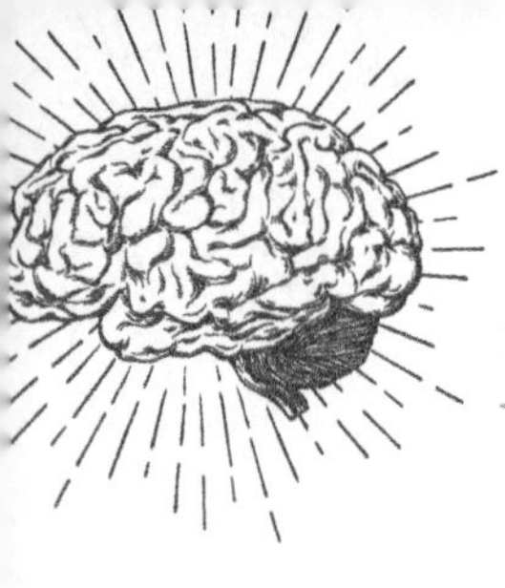

moral of the story is not "Never cross bridges." The moral is "Don't believe the claims of sketchy companies." The question of consent is much the same. People have to be truthful, and they have to be able to judge the truthfulness of others. As long as two people make good judgments about one another before engaging in sexual activity, there does not need to be an emotional bond before having sex.

According to this view, sex is a casual activity, much like dancing. Many people enjoy dancing with friends, acquaintances, or even strangers if they are in the right mood. Sex is different from dancing in that it usually involves nakedness and the exchange of bodily fluids. But if a person isn't shy about their body, and they know how to protect themselves, then the difference is trivial. In this view, sex does not require marriage or any significant relationship.

Philosopher David Benatar compared casual sex to "casual gastronomy" or "culinary promiscuity," in which one person may eat dinner with multiple friends, acquaintances, and strangers in the same week. Someone who does this is not condemned for "eating around." In the same way, a sexually promiscuous person should not be condemned for "sleeping around." Benatar granted that consent is necessary for all sexual interactions, but consent does not require emotional ties or commitment. Whether a person chooses one partner or multiple partners, there is no need for anything like the permanent loyalty that proponents of marriage envisioned. In fact, such loyalty might be smothering.

Benatar's Argument *FOR* Casual Sex

1. Sex is like eating (or skiing or dancing).
2. It is not wrong to have casual eating (or skiing or dancing) partners.
3. Therefore, it is not wrong to have casual sex partners.

Proponents of the significance view may grant the conclusion of the casual sex argument. But they may point out that, although it is morally permissible to have sex without an emotional connection, it is not *fulfilling*. Only a significant relationship will enable a couple to create sexual experiences that are truly satisfying for both individuals. For example, it is often more difficult for a woman to climax than it is for a man. In a casual sexual encounter, will a woman be able to convey what she needs, or will she have to go without being satisfied? She may prefer to be with someone who knows her well enough to facilitate her satisfaction.

Personal Statement

I had my first sexual experience when I was 17 years old. Growing up I was always told that sex was something that should only be done by married couples. For a little bit after that experience, I thought that I had done something wrong because I went against what

I was always told. Eventually, I realized that both my partner and I had a good time and that there was nothing wrong with what we did.

I still find sex to be something significant because I want to make sure that I'm having sex with someone who I emotionally resonate with; however, I don't feel bad giving myself to whomever I love at the time. Sex takes two people, but it is also very personal.

Make sure to have sex with people who agree to the same terms as you and to ensure consent. If you do decide to have sex, make sure to always practice safe sex and remember that your value as a person does not change no matter how many partners you decide to have.

Discussion Questions

1. What were you taught about sex as you were growing up? Which of these teachings were helpful? Which of them were not?
2. Which of the arguments in this chapter do you find most compelling? Why?
3. If a couple is dating, and one wishes to have sex before marriage while the other wishes to wait until marriage, how should they deal with the difference in opinion?
4. What other qualities could be used to determine if someone is ready for sex? Why?
5. Do you know when you will be ready for sex? When, if ever, do you think you will be ready?

Classroom Activities

1. Write and share stories about a world in which there is no such thing as marriage. What happens there?
2. Discuss your favorite songs about romantic love. What do these songs suggest about the connection between sex and emotion? Write and share your own poems or songs about romantic love.

References

Augustine of Hippo. (2012). *The works of Saint Augustine: A translation for the 21st century* (R. Teske, Trans.). New City Press. (Original work published 424)

Benatar, D. (2002). Two views of sexual ethics: Promiscuity, pedophilia, and rape. *Public Affairs Quarterly, 16*(3), 191–201.

Gilboa, D. (2002). Premarital sex and exploitation in a liberal society. *International Journal of Applied Philosophy, 16*(1), 55–67. https://doi.org/10.5840/ijap20021614

About the Author

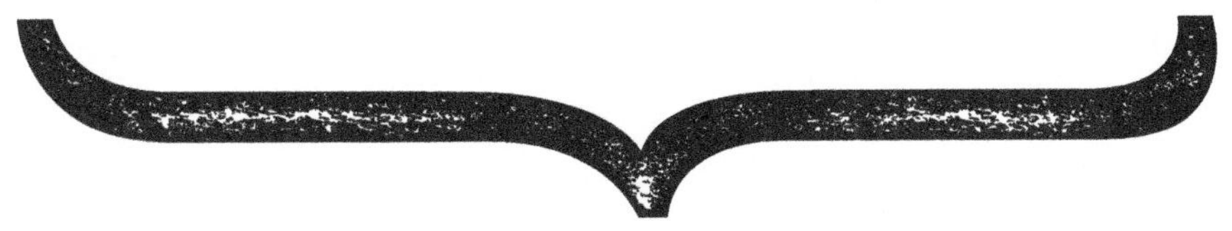

Sharon M. Kaye, Ph.D., is a professor in the Department of Philosophy at John Carroll University in Cleveland, OH. She graduated Phi Beta Kappa from the University of Wisconsin, Madison in 1992. After receiving her Ph.D. in 1997 from the University of Toronto, she was a Killam postdoctoral fellow at Dalhousie University in Halifax, Nova Scotia. Since then, she has published numerous articles as well as books, including *An Introduction to Eastern and Western Philosophy for Kids* (2020), *Philosophy for Teens* (2006) and *More Philosophy for Teens* (2007) with Paul Thomson, *Medieval Philosophy* (2008), *Black Market Truth* (2008), *Critical Thinking* (2009), *The Onion and Philosophy* (2010), *The Ultimate Lost and Philosophy* (2011), *What Philosophy Can Tell You About Your Lover* (2012), and *A Complete Introduction to Philosophy* (2014). Her works have been translated into Japanese, Greek, Turkish, Spanish, Portuguese, and Slovak. She is currently writing the K–12 philosophy curriculum for Royal Fireworks Press. She also directs a Philosophy for Kids Program that enables undergraduates to lead philosophy discussions for gifted middle school students. She has two children, two dogs, a cat, a gecko, and a fish.

About the Contributors

Dominic Fasano graduated from John Carroll University with a degree in philosophy and plans on going to graduate school. He is mainly interested in consciousness studies and philosophy of language. In his free time, you can find him at the shooting range, hitting the heavy bag, and playing fighting games.

Autumn Franz (she/her or they/them) is a recent graduate of John Carroll University with a bachelor's in sociology and gender, sexuality, and women's studies and a minor in philosophy. In their free time, Autumn loves to write poetry. They are passionate about LGBTQIA+ issues and relational health and enjoy educating others on these topics.

Maria Genova is a John Carroll graduate interested in the philosophical and literary movements of the late 19th and early 20th centuries. When she is not reading or at the park, she can be found playing with her two cats, Ichi and Miso.

Oliver Golias (they/them) is a philosophy student enrolled at the New School for Social Research in New York City. Their focus lies in how epistemological assumptions actualize in ethically and politically motivated actions. They wish to teach philosophy at the university level alongside activism work.

Tristan Hansen is a junior biology major at John Carrol University. He was born and raised in Cleveland, OH, and has a deep love for the city. He has a passionate thirst for knowledge that helps drive his love for philosophy. When he is not in deep philosophical thought, he enjoys spending time with his family and dog.

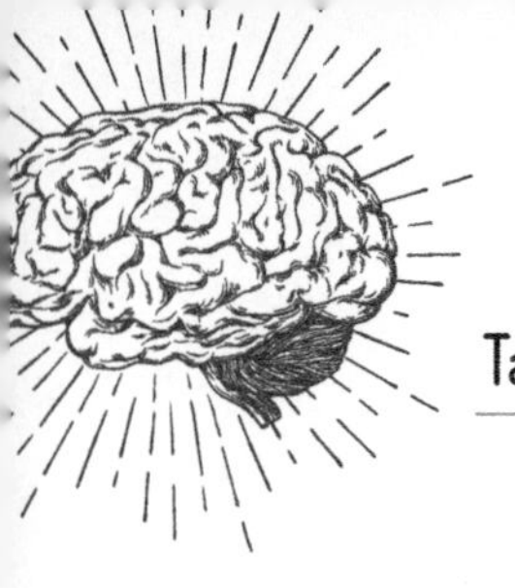

Celeste Johnson (they/them) is a philosophy and psychology double major at John Carroll University. They hope to go into the field of medicine in the future. They have also taught philosophy to fifth and sixth graders on numerous occasions. Their favorite philosopher is Simone de Beauvoir because they love existentialist philosophy and feminism.

Eric Johnston recently graduated from John Carroll University with a Bachelor of Science in business administration.

Tommy Kegler is a recent graduate from John Carroll University. He is currently pursuing a doctorate in political science with a focus on political theory at the University of California, Riverside.

Rachel C. Lee is an avid writer who loves to think about life's big questions. Although born in California, she grew up in Ohio and considers herself a Cleveland native. She recently finished her bachelor's in English at John Carroll University and lives with her parents and her beloved cat.

For Product Safety Concerns and Information please contact our EU representative GPSR@taylorandfrancis.com Taylor & Francis Verlag GmbH, Kaufingerstraße 24, 80331 München, Germany

Printed and bound by CPI Group (UK) Ltd, Croydon, CR0 4YY
08/06/2025
01896981-0004